POP-11:
A practical language for Artificial Intelligence

ELLIS HORWOOD SERIES IN COMPUTERS AND THEIR APPLICATIONS
Series Editor: Brian Meek, Director of the Computer Unit, Queen Elizabeth College, University of London

POP-11
A practical language for Artificial Intelligence

ROSALIND BARRETT, B.A.
ALLAN RAMSAY, B.Sc., M.Sc., Ph.D.
AARON SLOMAN, B.Sc., D.Phil.
all of Department of Cognitive Studies
School of Social Sciences
University of Sussex

ELLIS HORWOOD LIMITED
Publishers · Chichester

Halsted Press: a division of
JOHN WILEY & SONS
New York · Chichester · Brisbane · Toronto

First published in 1985 by

ELLIS HORWOOD LIMITED
Market Cross House, Cooper Street, Chichester, West Sussex, PO19 1EB, England

The publisher's colophon is reproduced from James Gillison's drawing of the ancient Market Cross, Chichester.

Distributors:

Australia, New Zealand, South-east Asia:
Jacaranda-Wiley Ltd., Jacaranda Press,
JOHN WILEY & SONS INC.,
G.P.O. Box 859, Brisbane, Queensland 4001, Australia

Canada:
JOHN WILEY & SONS CANADA LIMITED
22 Worcester Road, Rexdale, Ontario, Canada.

Europe, Africa:
JOHN WILEY & SONS LIMITED
Baffins Lane, Chichester, West Sussex, England.

North and South America and the rest of the world:
Halsted Press: a division of
JOHN WILEY & SONS
605 Third Avenue, New York, N.Y. 10158 U.S.A.

© 1985 R. Barrett, A. Ramsey and A. Sloman/Ellis Horwood Limited

British Library Cataloguing in Publication Data
Barrett, Rosalind
POP-11: a practical language for artificial intelligence. —
(Ellis Horwood series in computers and their applications)
1. POP-11 (Complete program language)
I. Title II. Ramsey, Allan, *1953–*
III. Sloman, Aaron

001.64'24 QA76.73.P/

ISBN 0—85312—940—1 (Ellis Horwood Limited — Library Edn.)
ISBN 0—85312—924—X (Ellis Horwood Limited — Student Edn.)
ISBN 0—470—20237—8 (Halsted Press)

Typeset by Ellis Horwood Limited
Printed in Great Britain by R.J. Acford, Chichester

Contents

Dedicated to the memory of Max Clowes

Preface

INTRODUCTION

POP-11 is a powerful general-purpose programming language. It is a descendant of POP-2, a language originally developed at Edinburgh University, named after one of its designers, Robin Popplestone.

Although developed for research and teaching in Artificial Intelligence, POP-11 is used for an increasing range of purposes including VLSI design, graphics, text processing, compiler design, image processing, expert system design, and design of tools for interactive program development.

This book, showing how to use the facilities provided in POP-11, is intended for a reader who already has programming experience in a conventional programming language, and will not be reading about procedures, variables, arguments, results, loops, stacks, etc. for the first time. Exercises have been included, with answers at the end of the book.

POP-11 — THE CORE OF POPLOG

POP-11 is the core of a large multi-language system called 'POPLOG', a name chosen when the system contained only POP-11 and PROLOG. POPLOG is used for teaching, research and development at a rapidly growing number of educational and industrial organisations. Only a very brief description of POPLOG is offered here. Later chapters will occasionally refer to the way the language POP-11 is integrated into the environment.

Initially developed in the Cognitive Studies Programme at Sussex University, since 1984 POPLOG has been marketed commercially by Systems Designers

International, and it has been adopted as part of the software infrastructure for the British Government's Alvey Programme. By early 1985 there were nearly 100 academic installations, and the number of industrial licences was approaching that number. It is being used not only in Britain but also in the USA, in several European countries, in Australia and in Sweden. There is a POPLOG User Group, run by Cambridge Consultants Ltd, in Cambridge, England.

POPLOG is an integrated, interactive, multi-language software development environment. Besides the core language POP-11, it contains incremental compilers for PROLOG (the logic programming language) and LISP, a versatile screen editor and other utilities. The editor, VED, is tailorable and provides a general-purpose, terminal independent user interface for screen-based programs, as well as being a powerful aid to program development, testing and documentation, and providing access to on-line help files, teaching files, and reference files.

Debates about the merits of programming languages are often ideological. The POPLOG designers believe different languages are good for different purposes. Moreover, huge investments in existing software cannot be discarded, so POPLOG provides integrated facilities for developing and mixing programs in different languages. For instance, PASCAL, FORTRAN or C programs may be linked dynamically into POPLOG, using the 'external load' mechanism.

Since the other incremental compilers and the editor are implemented in POP-11, it is worth knowing about it, even if it is not the main language used. Such knowledge makes it possible to take full advantage of facilities for extending and tailoring the environment. Moreover, for some tasks, such as programs which do a great deal of arithmetic, string or vector manipulation, or deterministic list processing, POP-11 is more convenient, and more efficient, than PROLOG.

POP-11 is similar to some of the more sophisticated versions of LISP, in that it provides a fully fledged research and development language, with a rich environment including incremental compiler, editor, on-line help mechanism, libraries, etc. Its syntax makes it more suitable as a teaching language than LISP, by reducing the cognitive load in reading programs. In particular, the richer, more redundant, syntax enables the compiler to produce more helpful syntactic error messages, since mismatched brackets can be more easily detected. For instance, here is a definition of one of the built-in procedures:

```
define max(num1, num2);    ;;; return the bigger of two numbers
    if      num1 > num2
    then    num1;
    else    num2;
    endif;
enddefine;
```

Similarly, there are separate opening and closing brackets for **for** loops and **while** loops, etc.

Why use POP-11 as a programming language rather than the better known languages like BASIC, FORTRAN, COBOL, C and PASCAL? For many purposes, POP-11 is a richer, more advanced language enabling more ambitious programs to be written with less effort. It enables the beginner to move quickly to more interesting projects. Like PASCAL, it encourages well-structured, clear programs made of independently testable parts. Like BASIC, LISP, LOGO and PROLOG, it is fully interactive, allowing full use of the computer to simplify and accelerate development and testing of programs. Unlike all others (apart from the biggest LISP sytems) it provides an elaborate but friendly environment with many built-in aids to program development and learning.

As with LISP systems, the incremental compiler and integrated editor VED can enormously speed up program development time. This is primarily because program editing, documentation, compiling, linking, testing, all use the same process rather than a separate editor, compiler, linker, and run-time debugger. Thus very little time is wasted switching contexts.

Like LISP, POP-11 can be used either as a main programming language or as an efficient systems language on which to build higher level tools, such as a logic programming language or an expert-system shell.

For declarative programs, and especially for tasks requiring depth-first search, PROLOG will often be a more suitable language. Therefore, POPLOG includes a full implementation of PROLOG, compatible with the DEC-10 version. POPLOG allows programs in POP-11 and PROLOG to be combined, where mixing is desirable. (See the on-line help files on PROLOG, if you have access to a POPLOG system. For an introduction to PROLOG, see *Programming in PROLOG* (1981) by W. Clocksin and C. Mellish, Springer-Verlag.)

For users wishing to produce a more integrated mix of POP-11 and logic programming, or for that matter users wishing to implement a new higher level language, appropriate system-building tools are provided within POP-11. These are the same tools as are used to build the existing compilers.

POP-11 is derived from POP-2, a language originally invented at Edinburgh University for research in Artificial Intelligence. POP-2 is described in *Programming in POP-2* (1971) by R. M. Burstall, J. S. Collins and R. J. Popplestone, Edinburgh University Press.

The original version of POP ran on an Elliot 4130 computer and is now obsolete. It was transferred to the DEC-10 computer running the TOPS-10 operating system in Edinburgh. Julian Davies, now at the University of Western Ontario, Canada, implemented an improved version, called POP-10, in the early seventies. A new version of POP for the DEC-10 called WPOP (WonderPOP), was implemented by Robert Rae and Allan Ramsay, and became available in the late seventies. It was also transferred to the TOPS-20 operating system.

Steve Hardy implemented the first version of POP-11 at Sussex University in 1975. This was a small system which ran on PDP-11 computers under the UNIX[†] operating system. It did not include all of POP-2, but had some extra features instead, designed to make it easier to use, especially for teaching purposes. In particular, the pattern matcher, the autoloadable library mechanism and a large collection of help and teaching files made it especially useful for educational purposes, and several universities and one school have been using it for some time. Some of its features were incorporated into WPOP.

†UNIX is a trade mark of Bell Laboratories.

That version of POP-11 is now obsolete, and Sussex University is no longer distributing it, but it may be possible to obtain a version which runs on PDP-11 computers with UNIX version 7, from Nottingham University Psychology Department. It includes only a subset of the current version of POP-11, and does not include the editor, VED.

The second version of POP-11, mostly implemented by John Gibson, first became available on VAX computers running VMS early in 1982, since when it has been substantially improved. It is much larger and has far more facilities than the earlier POP-11. It includes all the main features of POP-2 and many more. In particular, the core language was extended during 1983 to provide facilities to implement PROLOG more efficiently.

During 1983 the University of Sussex began to market POPLOG commercially, to universities and industrial organisations which required tools for Artificial Intelligence research and development. When it became clear that there was a substantial demand, marketing was taken over by Systems Designers International, Camberley, Surrey, England, apart from sales to UK academic institutions, which may still obtain it direct from the University of Sussex. Many users only discovered the virtues of POP-11 after acquiring POPLOG initially for one of the other languages.

During 1984/5 further facilities were added to support the implementation of COMMON LISP. These more advanced facilities are not described in this book.

The current POP-11 will run only on a computer which has a large address space, permitting processes of up to a megabyte in size or more, depending on how large user programs are. So it will not run on small personal computers or the PDP-11 family. However, as the price of hardware falls, we expect that within a few years it will be possible for computers in the home, in the office, and in schools to run systems as large as POP-11.

The new POP-11 is available only as part of POPLOG. It is designed to be portable and runs on VAX computers under VMS, Berkeley UNIX and Ultrix operating systems, on GEC Series 63 computers under AT&T UNIX System V, on M68000 computers (under Unisoft UNIX), and the SUN.2 workstation running Berkeley UNIX. Other implementations will be available later, including Hewlett Packard M68000 workstations running UNIX system III or System V. POP-11 can be used with an ordinary VDU with screen editing capabilities, but during 1985 it will also be linked to a window/mouse mechanism on the SUN workstation and other computers.

This book provides an introduction to the new larger version of POP-11. Many of the examples will also work on the smaller version, but not all.

POPLOG contains a powerful screen editor, VED, similar in many respects to EMACS. VED considerably reduces the effort involved in developing and testing programs, or writing documentation (this book would have taken many times longer to construct, had we not had VED available for running examples, recording their outputs, and then cut-and-pasting them into the main text). Ideally, before using POP-11 you should learn to use the screen editor.

Details of this editor will vary according to which terminals are available, so this book will not include information about the editor. If you have access to a computer running POPLOG you should ask for advice. There will be on-line documentation available which will show you how to use the editor on the terminals which are in use at your site.

An important feature of POP-11 is its inherent ability to be used in an 'on-line' mode. This means that commands in the language can be given at any time: there is no division between a phase in which you specify a program which is to be compiled, and a phase in which your programs run. You can interleave additions to the program and commands to run the program, using the same language and the same running process for both. Thus you can define a procedure, then run it to test it, then define a new procedure using the first one, then run it, then define new procedures, etc. If you find that a procedure needs to be changed you can edit it without leaving POP-11, and the new version will immediately be available without recompiling other procedures or relinking your program. For debugging purposes there is no need to invoke a separate interactive debugging tool providing a debugging command language. POP-11 itself is a very powerful interactive language which makes it possible to interrogate data structures or trace or untrace procedures while a program is running.

To make all this possible POP-11 contains an incremental compiler, which is part of the system when programs are running. In most languages the compiler is a separate program which runs to transform your program into machine language.

The use of an incremental compiler enables development and testing to be far more rapid than with a conventional programming language, such as PASCAL or FORTRAN. Some languages with an interpreter offer a similar facility (e.g. BASIC and LISP). The advantage of an incremental compiler over an interpreter is that it produces machine code, so that programs run faster. The advantage of using an interpreter is that it reads in programs faster, and can provide more flexible development aids.

Some programmers regard interactive program development as undisciplined. They assume the best method is to:

(1) specify the problem, or system requirements
(2) design programs and data structures required
(3) write the program
(4) compile the program
(5) run the program
(6) go back to (2) or (3) to fix 'bugs'

This method of using a computer is ideal when:

(a) the problem is well defined
(b) algorithms can be designed easily
(c) the user never makes a programming mistake
(d) the user is a perfect typist

If the last two conditions are not met then a slow and expensive iteration of steps (3) to (5) must be performed. Often even the first two conditions are not met. The problem may be well defined but so complex that initial algorithms do not cover all cases, or include inconsistencies or other errors, so that development and testing involves a slow iteration through steps (2) to (5). Sometimes even the problem is not very well defined, for instance where requirements for a program can only be developed as a result of running a prototype in the intended environment. In that case the iteration even involves step (1).

The conditions can sometimes be met, but not for complex problems or inexperienced users. An incremental compiler (or interpreter) with an integrated editor and other development aids can enormously speed up the process of producing and testing initial draft programs. Since each new portion of program can be tested quickly, without a slow process of relinking, an environment like that of POPLOG can encourage more thorough testing, leading to more reliable programs, as well as saving programmer effort. This is referred to as 'rapid prototyping'.

A consequence of using an incremental compiler is that there is not really any such thing as a program in POP-11. A conventional program consists of procedure definitions together with some commands invoking them and perhaps data files. The whole program has to be specified before any commands can be obeyed. In POP-11 you can go on indefinitely interleaving commands and new definitions. This encourages very thorough testing, and can usefully blur the distinction between development and use, allowing users to tailor a program to their needs.

In addition, like LISP, POP-11 does not require a separation of data and programs. We shall see how this provides powerful facilities, making it possible to mix factual assertions with program instructions.

Some languages make use of 'assertions', which can be used to give the computer information. For example, in PROLOG, the information 'tom is the father of dick' will be expressed by the assertion:

father(tom, dick).

They may also enable you to store generalisations, or inference rules. For example, in PROLOG the information 'x is the father of y if x is a parent of y and x is male', will be expressed by the assertion:

father(X,Y):− parent(X,Y), male(X).

Such languages also allow the construction of questions. For example, in PROLOG the question 'who is the father of joe?' will be expressed by the question:

?− father(X,joe).

These are examples of the 'declarative' style of programming.

POP-11 is not intended primarily for declarative programming, but there is a subject, called the 'database package', which provides something like assertions and questions. This package is built on more primitive list processing facilities.

Advocates of declarative languages sometimes suggest that logic programming should be used for all tasks. However, we need to think in terms of instructions as well as assertions and inference rules and this is why we have provided both in POPLOG. If someone asks you the way to the station, it will not usually be helpful to give lots of facts about the location. Instead you will probably give instructions such as 'go down that road until you come to the post office, then turn left . . .', and so on. If the questioner knows the town very well, it may suffice for them to be told 'the station is two blocks north of the post office'.

However, in order to make use of that information they will have to find some way of translating that into a plan for getting from where they are to the post office. A plan contains instructions about what to do when. Similarly, to make a computer do something other than answer factual questions you often need to be able to give it instructions.

Even if all you are interested in is storing information and getting answers to questions relating to the information, someone must first tell the computer how to store information, and how to respond to questions. Therefore instructions of some sort are required as the basis even for a purely declarative system.

POP-11, like many other languages, lacks the concept of a 'monitor' or 'demon' — a program which waits until some condition is satisfied and then immediately takes control and carries out its instructions. Thus you cannot say in POP-11 something like:

'if ever the value of X becomes 99 then print out a warning'.

It is possible, using advanced facilities in POP-11, to extend the language to allow such things. Such techniques will not be explained in this book. There are a few built-in special-purpose monitors, such as a user-definable procedure run whenever an error occurs, and another run whenever the user types an 'interrupt' character at the terminal.

Teach, Help and Ref files and the VED editor

The POPLOG system contains a very large number of **teach** files which are read using the VED editor. There are files covering the use of the editor VED, and its role in developing programs; files which provide a succession of mini-projects, for the absolute beginner with no experience of programming; files which cover various aspects of POP-11; and files which cover various topics in AI in some depth, with exercises and projects. If you have access to a POPLOG system then typing

```
teach teachfiles
```

will get you a summary of these files, telling you what they are about and who they are appropriate for.

There are also a large number of more technical files available. The **help** command also invokes VED, for reading shorter files describing POP-11 facilities. For an overview of **help** files type:

```
help contents
```

Use 'explain' if VED has not been tailored for your terminal:

```
explain contents
```

The ref command may be used to access files which give a definitive description of POP-11 and its main system utilities.

Readers will benefit from having access to POPLOG. This book therefore includes occasional references to help or teach files which may be useful. Readers without access to POPLOG may ignore such references.

Chapter 1 describes in some detail an example which illustrates how to use POP-11 as a list-processing language with a conventional syntax. Later chapters provide more general descriptions of the language and some of its most useful facilities. Towards the end of the book more powerful mechanisms are described.

ACKNOWLEDGEMENTS

This book was produced by Rosalind Barrett and Allan Ramsay, working from a draft introduction to POP-11 produced by Aaron Sloman, based in part on portions of the on-line help and teach files written by many other members of the Cognitive Studies Programme at Sussex University, especially Max Clowes, John Gibson and Steve Hardy. Steve Isard, in the Experimental Psychology Laboratory at Sussex University, also helped with some of the original files, as did Chris Mellish and Jonathan Cunningham. John Williams, Jonathan Laventhol, Mark Rubenstein, Tom Khabaza and David Allport annotated sections of the final draft. Suggestions and comments were made by various students, visitors and staff including Graham Brown, Phil Philpot and Kim Hawksworth of Systems Designers Ltd, Sak Wathanasin, and Leila Burrell-Davis.

The Science and Engineering Research Council and the Alvey Directorate provided support for POPLOG, and GEC Research Laboratories provided a research Fellowship for Aaron Sloman during 1984–86.

1

A detailed worked example

1.1 INTRODUCTION

This chapter presents a simple program worked out in some detail by way of an introduction to POP-11. More general and complete explanations of all the issues raised are given in later chapters, along with more sophisticated techniques that could have been used. Ideally the reader should try out the example on a computer running POPLOG, but, for readers with some programming experience, it should be intelligible without that.

POP-11 allows upper and lower case letters to be used, and they are distinguished. Most POP-11 key words, for example, define and if, are lower case. We will use this typeface for all POP-11 examples in this book.

1.2 THE ROOMS EXERCISE

Suppose we have the dimensions of a set of rooms in a building. We might want programs to print out various kinds of information about the rooms, such as the perimeters, floor areas and volumes. To illustrate a number of basic features of POP-11, we define a collection of procedures to perform such tasks.

First we must give POP-11 information about the set of rooms. We can declare a variable called rooms, and then represent the information for each room as a list containing the room name, its length, breadth and height. (A list is a powerful data structure used to represent information.) We can then represent information about the set of rooms as a list of lists. Finally, we can ask POP-11 to assign the list of lists to the variable rooms:

```
vars rooms;
[[room1 10 12 8]
 [room2 6 11 8]
 [room3 15 11 8]
 [room4 10 12 9]
 [room5 21 11 9]] -> rooms;
```

The occurrence of a pair of square brackets [. . .] tells POP-11 to construct a list. Nesting the brackets tells POP-11 to make a list of lists. The $->$ is the assignment arrow. Whatever appears on the left-hand side of it becomes the value of the variable on the right of it.

POP-11's lexical analysis rules say that a word starting with a letter may include a digit, so that room1 is accepted as a single word, not a word and a digit, whereas 1room would have been split into a number and a word, that is, 1 and room.

We have declared rooms as a 'global' variable. That is, it is not declared inside any procedure, unlike some of the 'local' variables introduced below. This means that it can be referred to at any time, and its value altered, or used, or printed out. For example, we can give a command to print it out using the 'pretty-print' arrow ==>:

```
rooms ==>
```

The pretty-print arrow tells POP-11 to print two stars (**) and then to print the specified object in a legible format, as in:

```
** [[room1 10 12 8]
    [room2 6 11 8]
    [room3 15 11 8]
    [room4 10 12 9]
    [room5 21 11 9]]
```

We now define a top level procedure, which takes a list of lists like that above as input, then for each embedded list extracts the name, the length, the breadth and the height, and prints out the name followed by the perimeter, area and volume. We define this top level procedure, called display_data, below. It uses two local variables, list_of_lists, to hold the complete list of information given as input to the procedure, and room, to refer to the data for each room in turn:

```
define display_data(list_of_lists);
    vars room;
    for room in list_of_lists do
        display_room(room);
    endfor;
enddefine;
```

This tells POP-11 that we are defining a new procedure. The first line says that the procedure is called display_data; it will be applied to one object, known as the input, which, within the procedure, will be called list_of_lists. We can call the object anything else in other places: the name, or variable, is private, or 'local', to the procedure. In fact, we shall see that the global variable rooms can be given as input to display_data, but so could other lists of information so long as they were in the same format.

The second line declares an additional local variable called room. room is used to retrieve information about individual rooms from list_of_lists.

The next three lines use the imperative construction

```
for ... in ... do ... endfor;
```

which enables a program to take each element of a list in turn and do something to it. The local variable room refers initially to the first element of the list, then the second, then the third, and so on. It does not matter how long the list is; each element will be dealt with in turn. The instruction display_room(room); applies the procedure display_room to whatever is referred to by room. We define display_room later. display_room is called once for each element of the list called list_of_lists. When display_room has been applied to the last element of list_of_lists, the procedure stops since there is no instruction after the word endfor. endfor signals the end of the 'for loop'. The word enddefine signals the end of a procedure definition.

We now have to define the procedure display_room. Look back at the list of information assigned to the global variable rooms. We want to apply display_room to each element of that list in turn. Each element is a list of four elements — a word, which is a room name, followed by three numbers. So we define display_room to cope with such a four element list as its input.

Using the built-in printing procedure pr, and procedures we have yet to define for computing perimeter, area and volume, we could define the procedure like this:

```
define display_room(list);
    ;;; print out information about the room given in list
    vars room_name, room_length, room_width, room_height;
    list(1) -> room_name;
    list(2) -> room_length;
    list(3) -> room_width;
    list(4) -> room_height;
    pr('INFORMATION CONCERNING '); pr(room_name);
    pr(newline);
    pr('  The perimeter is ');
    pr(perim(room_length, room_width));
    pr(' feet');
    pr(newline);
    pr('  The area is ');
    pr(area(room_length, room_width));
    pr(' square feet');
    pr(newline);
    pr('  The volume is ');
    pr(volume(room_length, room_width, room_height));
    pr(' cubic feet');
    pr(newline);
enddefine;
```

Let us look at the definition in detail. The first line says that we are defining a procedure called display_room. It takes one input argument, known as list within the procedure. The second line is a comment, and is ignored by POP-11, but may be useful to the user. Comments enable other people to understand your programs when they have to repair or upgrade them when you are not there. They enable you to understand your programs when you come to repair or upgrade them some time after you wrote them. POP-11 provides two formats for writing comments. The one we have used here, and which we will use frequently throughout this book, is the 'end of line comment'. Anything to the right of a sequence of three semicolons is ignored by the POP-11 compiler, so you can leave reminders about what each line of your program is for by including ;;; and then some explanatory remarks. Longer comments, extending over several lines, are marked by the 'comment brackets' /* and */, so that

```
/* This is a comment which
appears on two lines */
```

would also be ignored by the compiler. The next line declares four local variables:

```
vars room_name, room_length, room_width, room_height;
```

The next line

```
list(1) -> room_name;
```

is an instruction to take the first element in the object called list and assign it to the variable room_name. Once we have assigned this item to room_name, we can retrieve it simply by asking for the value of room_name. This is more convenient than repeatedly asking for the first element of list. The remaining items in the information list are treated similarly.

Notice that the expression list(1) can be used to refer to the first element of a list. Similarly, list(2) refers to the second element, and so on.

The next line of the definition contains two instructions to print information:

```
pr('information concerning '); pr(room_name);
```

The first prints the sequence of characters in between the string quotes, '. . .'; a character may be a space. The second prints the value of the variable room_name, which will be a word, for example room1 or room2. The instruction

```
pr(newline);
```

causes a new line to be printed. The next line

```
pr(' the perimeter is ');
```

causes the sequence of characters between the string quotes to be printed out. The next instruction

```
pr(perim(room_length, room_width));
```

gives the values of room_length and room_width to a procedure called perim (not yet defined). perim produces one result which is then given as input to the procedure pr. pr prints the result out. For example, if room_length has the value 10, and room_width has the value 12, perim returns 44, which pr prints. Here we are using the expression

perim(room_length, room_width);

to refer to the number which is the perimeter of the room. So, when we define the procedure called perim, we have to ensure that it produces a result, that is, something which can be used by this sort of expression.

The remainder of our procedure, display_room, uses similar techniques, first using a procedure area, which has yet to be defined, then a procedure volume, also to be defined. Note that the instruction

pr(volume(room_length, room_width, room_height));

in display_room takes three input arguments, not two like the others.

Below is how you might define perim to calculate a perimeter. It takes two numbers, adds them, and then multiplies the result by 2. The total is the result of the procedure:

```
define perim(len, breadth) -> total;
    (len + breadth) * 2 -> total;
enddefine;
```

The first line has two new features. First, perim takes not one, but two input variables — len and breadth. (We cannot use the word length for the first argument, as it is the name of a POP-11 system procedure. Using length will produce an error resulting in a mishap message — hence we use len.) Second, the procedure header ends with —> total; this says that perim produces one result. What that result is depends on what is assigned to the variable total in the procedure.

—> total in the header is not itself an assignment. It indicates how to use the variable total in the procedure. That is, it is an 'output local' variable, whereas len and breadth are 'input locals'. Although the output local declaration looks like an assignment, it does not cause the procedure to assign anything to the variable. Rather, it indicates that after the procedure is used there will be a result available, and the user must take care to assign something to the variable total within the procedure, to be used as the result.

We can test the procedure using ==> to print out the result:

```
perim(3, 5) ==>
** 16
```

Actually, the pretty-print arrow, ==>, is not needed for printing out something as simple as a number. It is intended for printing more complex structures, like lists of lists. So in this case we could use the ordinary print arrow, =>. Output produced by the ordinary print arrow is also preceded by **. For example:

```
perim(3, 5) =>
** 16
```

We can define area and volume similarly

```
define area(len, breadth) -> total;
    len * breadth -> total;
enddefine;
```

and test it:

```
area(8, 12) =>
** 96

define volume(len, breadth, height) -> total;
    len * breadth * height -> total;
enddefine;


volume(5, 5, 5) =>
** 125
```

Now that we have defined all the procedures that display_room needs, we can test display_room itself, remembering that it requires a list of information about one room. For example, the command

```
display_room([room5 21 11 9]);
```

prints out the following:

```
INFORMATION CONCERNING room5
    The perimeter is 64 feet
    The area is 231 square feet
    The volume is 2079 cubic feet
```

Notice that since display_room does not make use of the list rooms, it can take any four element list as input (so long as the last three elements are numbers), for example:

```
display_room([room17 5 6 7]);
```

We can now run the top level procedure on the list rooms, which we created above. Just to check, we can print out the contents of the list

```
rooms ==>
** [[room1 10 12 8]
    [room2 6 11 8]
    [room3 15 11 8]
    [room4 10 12 9]
    [room5 21 11 9]]
```

and then run the top level procedure, giving it the list rooms as input:

```
display_data(rooms);
```

This prints the following:

```
INFORMATION CONCERNING room1
   The perimeter is 44 feet
   The area is 120 square feet
   The volume is 960 cubic feet
INFORMATION CONCERNING room2
   The perimeter is 34 feet
   The area is 66 square feet
   The volume is 528 cubic feet
INFORMATION CONCERNING room3
   The perimeter is 52 feet
   The area is 165 square feet
   The volume is 1320 cubic feet
INFORMATION CONCERNING room4
   The perimeter is 44 feet
   The area is 120 square feet
   The volume is 1080 cubic feet
INFORMATION CONCERNING room5
   The perimeter is 64 feet
   The area is 231 square feet
   The volume is 2079 cubic feet
```

It is worth noting that only one of our procedures does any printing, display_room. The procedures perim, area, and volume produce results which they do not print out themselves. display_room uses the results and prints them. The results can also be used for other purposes. For instance, below is an alternative version of the procedure volume. It takes three inputs. The procedure area uses two of them and the result is multiplied by the value of the variable height:

```
define volume(len, breadth, height) -> total;
    area(len, breadth) * height -> total;
enddefine;
```

Exercises

The above example illustrates features of POP-11 which are explained in more detail later on. The following exercises should test your understanding so far.

1. Modify the program so that in addition to the information shown above, the dimensions of each room are printed out, before the perimeter. You will need to work out which procedure should be modified, and how to modify it. All the techniques required have already been demonstrated.
2. Explain what the for . . . endfor loop form achieves.
3. Where are local variables declared? Where are global variables declared?
4. To the left of the assignment arrow in the imperative

    ```
    area(len, breadth) * height -> total;
    ```

    there are five expressions denoting numbers. What are they?
5. Explain the difference between —> in a procedure heading and in an assignment instruction. (More on this later.)

Searching for information

In our example so far, we have used all the information in the list rooms in a rather verbose fashion. The information about room5 could have been retrieved by using our knowledge of the order of the items in the list rooms. We could access the fifth element and give it to display_room using the expression rooms(5). For example, the command

```
display_room(rooms(5));
```

prints out:

```
INFORMATION CONCERNING room5
   The perimeter is 64 feet
   The area is 231 square feet
   The volume is 2079 cubic feet
```

If we do not know the order in which the information is stored, we can define a procedure to search rooms for information about a specific room. We want a procedure called findroom which:

(i) takes a room name and a list of room data as input
(ii) produces the data for the given room as its result.

findroom, below, achieves this. It examines each piece of room information in turn until the one whose first element is the name of the required room is found. At that point the search stops. If the room is not found, a mishap message is printed out.

Do not worry if you do not understand everything in the definition of findroom. This is just to give you a feel for the later chapters on list processing, conditionals and looping constructs.

```
define findroom(name, list_of_lists) -> room;
    ;;; search list_of_lists for one starting with NAME
    for room in list_of_lists do
        if room(1) = name then
            return();  ;;; terminate procedure
        endif;
    endfor;
    ;;; produce a MISHAP message
    mishap('ROOM NOT FOUND', [^name ^list_of_lists]);
enddefine;
```

findroom uses a for <item> in <list> do <action> endfor loop. This time the <action> is a conditional expression of the form:

```
if <condition> then <action> endif
```

Later we will meet other forms of conditionals. The <action> in this case is simply to return, that is, to terminate executing the current procedure. room is an output local. Thus the result of findroom is the list of information about the room whose name matches the input local variable name.

We give findroom the name of a room, and a list of lists of rooms as input. The name of the room must be in word quotes, ". . .". This means that the actual word, rather than its value, will be searched for in the list of lists. For example:

```
findroom("room3", rooms) =>
** [room3 15 11 8]

findroom("room5", rooms) =>
** [room5 21 11 9]
```

If you give findroom a non-existent room a mishap message is printed:

```
findroom("room17", rooms) =>

;;; MISHAP - ROOM NOT FOUND
;;; INVOLVING:   room17 [[room1 10 12 8] [room2 6 11 8]
         [room3 15 11 8] [room4 10 12 9] [room5 21 11 9]]
;;; DOING     :   findroom compile
```

or

```
findroom(room3, rooms) =>
;;; DECLARING VARIABLE room3

;;; MISHAP - ROOM NOT FOUND
;;; INVOLVING:   <undef room3> [[room1 10 12 8] [room2 6 11 8]
         [room3 15 11 8] [room4 10 12 9] [room5 21 11 9]]
;;; DOING     :   findroom compile
```

In this last example, the word quotes around room3 were omitted, so findroom tried to find a room whose name was whatever was the value of room3, rather than room3 itself.

findroom is sufficiently general to be given different lists of rooms on different occasions. We can use it to define a procedure called find_and_show, below, to print out the data concerning a given room. It uses findroom to dig out the list of data for display_room to print:

```
define find_and_show(name, list);
    display_room(findroom(name, list));
enddefine;
```

Notice that the two items given as input to find_and_show are simply handed on as input to findroom. findroom produces a result which is used as input for display_room. The same procedure could be written less compactly, though perhaps more clearly, using a local variable to hold the result produced by findroom.

```
define find_and_show(name, list);
    vars room;
    findroom(name, list) -> room;
    display_room(room);
enddefine;
```

To test the procedure, we can type:

```
find_and_show("room2", rooms);
```

This prints the following:

```
INFORMATION CONCERNING room2
    The perimeter is 34 feet
    The area is 66 square feet
    The volume is 528 cubic feet
```

Notice that find_and_show does not produce a result, since it has no output local. Because of this we do not use the print arrow when calling it. Instead, the semicolon terminates the imperative.

Finding several rooms

If we wanted to dig out information about not just one room, but about several, we could define a procedure to take a list of the names of wanted rooms, as well as the list of room data, and search for each required room in turn using find_and_show. This is what the procedure find_and_show_all, below, does:

```
define find_and_show_all(namelist, list);
    vars name;
    for name in namelist do find_and_show(name, list); endfor;
enddefine;
```

To test find_and_show_all with two rooms to search for in our global list rooms, we can type:

```
find_and_show_all([room2 room4], rooms);
```

This produces:

```
INFORMATION CONCERNING room2
    The perimeter is 34 feet
    The area is 66 square feet
    The volume is 528 cubic feet
INFORMATION CONCERNING room4
    The perimeter is 44 feet
    The area is 120 square feet
    The volume is 1080 cubic feet
```

You may already be able to see that we can define procedures which are much more flexible than this. In this example, we always dig out the same sort of information, even though it may be about different rooms. We could define procedures which produce different sorts of information. For example, given a width, find all the rooms with that width, or find all the rooms which have a given length and height, and so on. Later we shall see that use of the POP-11 matcher would make this sort of flexibility much easier to achieve.

Exercises

6. Modify the above examples to define a procedure called findroom_len which, instead of being given the name of a room, is given its length. It should print out information about all rooms with that length.

7. The procedure find_and_show_all could be very inefficient. For each room name it initiates a new search all the way down the list, using find_and_show. If the list of room data is very long, this could be very wasteful. Try defining a new version of find_and_show_all which is essentially like findroom, but modified to take a list of names instead of just one name. Further, it would not have an output local, since it would print relevant information instead of producing a result. Two further modifications of findroom will be needed. The call of mishap at the end should be removed, and the conditional

```
if room(1) = name then
     return();         ;;; stop the procedure
endif;
```

will need to be replaced by something equivalent to the following (which is not POP-11):

```
if room(1) is a member of the list of names then
    display_room(room);
endif;
```

There is a standard POP-11 procedure, called member, for testing whether some item is a member of a list. So you could use a conditional starting something like:

```
if member(room(1), namelist) then
```

2

Syntax and semantics of POP–11

Any programming language has two main aspects: the syntax, or symbolic structures, and their semantics, or meanings. In this chapter we introduce the details of the syntax and semantics of POP-11. It is a more formal introduction than Chapter 1, extending in more general terms some of the constructs illustrated there.

In POP-11 there are two sorts of syntactic structures with different sorts of meanings — there are expressions, which refer to objects, and imperatives, which refer to actions. To describe POP-11 we need to specify what sorts of objects there are, and what sorts of actions can be performed on them. We also need to define the syntax for creating or referring to objects, and for specifying or performing actions.

Some actions are concerned entirely with processes within the computer, for example, re-ordering a list of names. Others may be concerned with information flowing into or out of the computer, for example text read in from, or printed out to, the terminal or a disc file. We concentrate on the former type of action in this chapter.

2.1 SOME POP-11 DATA TYPES

Objects referred to in POP-11 include numbers, words, strings and lists. (We introduce others later.) There are standard notations in POP-11 for referring to these simple data types:

Numbers:

> Integers: 66   99876789   −66
>
> Decimals: 88.532   1.2345e3 (=1234.5)   123.4e−3 (=0.1234)

Words:

> "cat"   "ninety"   "count_num"   "+"   "+**+"   "if"   "IF"

Strings:

> 'cat'   'ninety'   '66'   'a string with spaces +**ƌƌƌƌ'

Lists:

> [a list of words]   [[a list] [of lists] [66 77]]

POP-11 also provides several other data types, see Tables 2.2 and 2.3, and allows the user to define new ones.

2.2 SOME POP-11 ACTIONS

Imperatives produce actions in POP-11. Actions may create objects, compare them, search for them, store them, print them out, and so on. There are many forms of imperatives for different purposes. For example, here is a command to print out the sum of two numbers:

```
99 + 66 =>
** 165
```

and here is a command to store a number in the variable num; it is an assignment:

```
66 -> num;
```

The assignment arrow, −>, should be read as 'goes to'. POP-11 differs from most programming languages in that assignment goes from left to right: first specify the object to be assigned, then say where it is to be stored.

In fact, all expressions can be regarded as imperatives since the objects that they refer to (directly or indirectly) have to be found or constructed. For example, the expression 3 + 4 refers to the object 7. Arriving at the number 7 involves doing an addition.

2.3 BUILT-IN AND USER-DEFINED PROCEDURES

POP-11 has many different sorts of built-in instructions, and users may define new ones. In POP-11 these are called 'procedures'. The user defines POP-11 procedures by providing a procedure name followed by instructions; the instructions are obeyed when the procedure name is used as part of an imperative.

There are different ways of putting instructions together. One common way is just to write them down as a sequence of things to be done in order.

Another form is as a conditional expression; what is done in this case depends upon the result of one or more tests. Instructions can also be put together using looping constructs (often referred to as 'iterations'); here a set of instructions is obeyed repeatedly until some terminating condition is reached.

2.4 COMMENTS IN POP-11 PROGRAMS

You will find that inserting short explanatory passages (often only a single line) helps explain a piece of POP-11 program (either to someone else who has to do something to it, or to yourself when you come back to it after you have not worked on it for a while and have forgotten how it works). POP-11 provides two ways in which you can add comments to your programs.

You can add short comments by including three consecutive semicolons. Anything to the right of these semicolons on the same line will be skipped by the POP-11 compiler. For example:

```
;;; This is a comment
3 + 5 =>      ;;; Print sum of 3 and 5
** 8
```

Longer comments may be included between the comment brackets, /* and */, as in:

```
/*
This is a long comment, going over several lines, which is
enclosed between the comment brackets /* and */. Note that it
includes a nested pair of comment brackets
*/
```

We make frequent use of comments throughout this book. All such text is completely ignored by the POP-11 compiler.

2.5 BOOLEAN EXPRESSIONS

Truth values in POP-11 are represented by the boolean objects <true> and <false>. (They are named after the logician George Boole.) The variables true and false have the boolean objects as their values. For example:

```
true =>
** <true>

false =>
** <false>
```

When we refer to boolean objects in our text, we will write true or false when we are talking about things which you would give a procedure as arguments (since this is how you would write them if you wanted to specify them explicitly). We will write <true> or <false> when we are talking about things that a procedure would return as results (since this is how they would be printed by the system if you called such a procedure and asked for its result to be printed).

POP–11 provides a number of built-in procedures, such as the infix operators = and <, which evaluate their arguments and return boolean objects, as shown below:

```
"town" = "town" =>   ;;; is "town" the same as "town"?
** <true>

3 < 1 =>             ;;; is 3 smaller than 1?
** <false>
```

Booleans are used in conditional instructions and in tests for the termination of loops. <true> is returned by all truth testing procedures when an expression does not evaluate to <false>. In conditional expressions, and tests for termination of loops, anything other than the item <false> is taken to mean <true>. For example:

```
        if 6 then "yes" => endif;
        ** yes
```

2.6 ERRORS AND ERROR MESSAGES

When you type something that the machine cannot understand, it will respond by printing out a mishap message. For example, if you leave out the + between two numbers, as in

```
    6 6 =>
```

the machine will react by printing out:

```
;;; MISHAP – MSEP: MISSING SEPARATOR (eg semicolon)
;;; INVOLVING: 6 6
;;; DOING    : compile
```

The 'code' before the colon in the top line (MSEP in this case) is a key to a help file which will explain in more detail what this sort of error message is about. You can examine the relevant explanatory file with the command:

```
help msep
```

This will invoke the POP-11 help facility. Alternatively, the command

```
explain msep
```

prints the explanatory file.

Syntactic and semantic errors

Some mistakes are 'syntactic', or 'compile time', errors. These occur when you type what POP-11 regards as meaningless instructions. The MISSING SEPARA-

TOR error, above, is an example. 'Semantic', or 'run time', errors occur when POP-11 understands the instructions, but discovers in the course of obeying them that something is wrong, for example:

```
"one" + "two" =>     ;;; POP-11 cannot add words

;;; MISHAP - NUMBER(S) NEEDED
;;; INVOLVING:  one two
;;; DOING    :  + compile
```

POP-11 understood that it was being told to add two things, so it invoked the procedure +. This procedure checked the input arguments. When it discovered that they were words it invoked the error handler to print the mishap message. POP-11 only knows how to add numbers. Notice that the DOING line mentions that it was actually doing +, as well as compile. In the previous case it was only doing compile.

In order to do anything, POP-11 has first to read in characters up to either a semicolon or a print arrow. What you type in is compiled, that is, your commands are translated into machine instructions, and then obeyed. In our example above, POP-11 invoked compile, which invoked the procedure + to do something. It was in the middle of doing both + and (temporarily suspended) compile, when the error occurred. The sequence of procedure calls is illustrated below:

POP-11 runs compile, which reads your commands, so
　　　　compile calls +
　　　　　　　+ calls the error procedure mishap

After the error the system goes back to reading in commands.

It is a good idea to include calls of mishap in your own programs, so that when things go wrong you are informed about it. The format of a call of mishap is

```
mishap(<error message>, <list of culprits>)
```

The <error message> should be a string describing what was wrong. The <list of culprits> should contain the collection of items which were found to be unsuitable. Calls of mishap are usually embedded in conditional expressions, for example:

```
unless  isinteger(n)
then    mishap('INTEGER REQUIRED', [% n %]);
endunless;
```

If this expression were to be evaluated before n had been given a value (so it was not an integer), the following message would be printed out:

```
;;; MISHAP - INTEGER REQUIRED
;;; INVOLVING:  <undef n>
;;; DOING    :  compile
Setpop
```

Including calls of mishap in your programs will make them much easier to debug, since you will be able to pinpoint where things are going wrong very precisely. You will need to make use of the facilities described in Section 5.3 for making up lists, in order to construct the list of culprits using the percent symbol, %, as in the example. How mishap works, and how you can change its behaviour, is described in Section 13.4.

2.7 EXPRESSIONS: SOME EXAMPLES

Before explaining how to define procedures, we need to explain some more about the building blocks, namely expressions and imperatives. We need expressions to tell POP-11 which objects to manipulate. Among the objects we can manipulate are numbers, words and lists. Here are some POP-11 expressions which denote numbers:

```
3
999
999 + 5
(999 + 5) - 666
```

Here is an imperative which contains an expression 999 + 5 and, using the print arrow, tells POP-11 to print out what the expression denotes:

```
999 + 5 =>
** 1004
```

Here are some expressions denoting a list of words, a list of three lists of words, and a list of numbers:

```
[a list of five words]
[[a dog] [an orange cat called marmaduke] [esther and mike]]
[1 2 3 4 5 6 7 8 9]
```

You can mix words and numbers, as in:

```
[1 2 3 4 5 6 7 8 9 10 jack queen king]
```

This denotes a list containing the numbers from 1 to 10, together with the words "jack", "queen", "king". More precisely, it is an instruction to POP-11 to create list containing these items. If you type the same thing again it will create another similar list, containing the same items.

You can also have an empty list, denoted by [ ] . This empty list is kept as the value of the variable nil. We can compare them to check:

```
[] = nil =>
** <true>
```

Lists are very flexible since they can contain arbitrarily many things. Later we shall see many examples of the use of lists to group things together.

To sum up: an expression is a piece of POP-11 which refers to some object. It may be an object which always exists, for example the number 99, or it may be an object created as a result of the use of the expression, for example a list of numbers. In order to do something to such an object it is necessary to use an imperative which tells POP-11 to perform some action on it.

2.8 IMPERATIVES: SOME EXAMPLES

We give more examples of commonly used imperatives below.

Two forms of print arrow

POP-11 provides several means of printing information so that it goes to the terminal, into a file, into the editor buffer, or into a data structure. One of the most commonly used is the print arrow, which we have seen previously. There are two versions of this:

> => (ordinary print arrow)
> This prints everything 'on the stack', preceded by **, unless called from inside a procedure, in which case it prints out only the top item of the stack, preceded by **. We will have more to say about the stack later. For now, think of => as printing out the 'unused' results of previously executed procedures.

> ==> (pretty-print arrow)
> This prints out only one object. If the object is a list or a vector, and if printing it out would take more than one line, the object is printed in a special format using indentation to make its structure clearer.

Examples:

```
33 + 66 => ;;; print sum of 33 and 66
** 99

234 + 22  >  33 * 66  => ;;; is 234 + 22 bigger than 33 times 66?
** <false>

99 + 5 = 95 + 9  => ;;; is 99 + 5 equal to 95 + 9?
** <true>


10 // 3 => ;;; divide 10 by 3 and print out  remainder and quotient
** 1 3
```

When lists are deeply nested the form printed out by => can be a little confusing, so it is then best to use ==> instead. You can, in fact, always use ==>. It is especially useful for a list of several lists of similar format, for example, a list of lists of information about people:

```
[
    [the mother of mary is suzy]
    [the father of mary is joe]
    [the mother of joe is miranda]
    [the father of joe is fred]
] ==>

** [[the mother of mary is suzy]
    [the father of mary is joe]
    [the mother of joe is miranda]
    [the father of joe is fred]]
```

Using => would have produced:

```
** [[the mother of mary is suzy] [the father of mary is joe]
    [the mother of joe is miranda] [the father of joe is fred]]
```

Note that => and ==> can be used to terminate an imperative without a semicolon.

Other printing procedures

POP-11 provides a number of built-in procedures for printing things in a more controlled format than the print arrows. In particular, the procedures pr and spr print things without starting a new line or printing the asterisks **. The difference between them is that spr prints a space after printing its argument. So

```
pr("cat"); pr("mouse"); spr("hat"); spr("coat");
```

prints:

```
catmousehat coat
```

Using the built-in printing procedures, it is fairly easy in POP-11 to define your own procedures to print things out in whatever format you like.

2.9 ASSIGNMENT

Another common form of imperative is an assignment, using the assignment arrow ->. Here is how you assign numbers as the values of the variables x and y:

```
99 -> x;
```

```
99 + 5 -> y;
```

In both cases the left-hand side is an expression which denotes a number. The whole thing says 'take the thing denoted by the expression on the left, and make the thing on the right (the variable x or y) refer to it from now on'. Thus, in the second example, y will refer to 104. This can be shown by another imperative:

```
y =>
** 104
```

Normally an imperative which does not end with the print arrow, =>, must end with a semicolon. Later we will see that if an imperative is embedded in a larger structure it does not always need the semicolon. A few more examples of assignments follow:

To give the variable y twice the value of x do:

```
x + x -> y;
```

Notice the difference between putting the variable on the left and on the right of an assignment. On the left its existing value is used. On the right a new value is set, or assigned. So to assign the value of x to y do:

```
x -> y;
```

To assign a list of numbers to list1, do something like:

```
[1 2 3 4 5]  -> list1;
```

To assign a list like list1, but in reverse order, to x, do:

```
rev(list1)  -> x; x =>
** [5 4 3 2 1]
```

rev is a built-in procedure which, when given a list as argument, produces a new list with the same elements in reverse order.

2.10 DECLARATIONS USING VARS

Declarations may be used to introduce new variable names. For example

```
vars x, y;
```

declares to POP-11 that you wish to use the names x and y as names for objects. The comma is optional. Any number of variables may be introduced in one declaration. The same syntax is used for introducing both global variables and local variables, explained below.

Variables may be used without being declared. This is equivalent to declaring them globally, except that POP-11 prints out a warning message:

```
3 -> xx;
;;; DECLARING VARIABLE xx        (Printed by POP-11)
```

If you declare a variable which is already part of the POP-11 system vocabulary, for example

```
vars define;
```

you will get a mishap message. Redeclaring one of your own variables has no effect. A vars declaration is an instruction to the compiler to enter the specified word in the system's dictionary of identifiers. If it is already there, there is no need to enter it. Redeclaring a variable does not overwrite its current value, for example:

```
vars n;                     ;;; Declare N as a variable
3 -> n;                     ;;; Give it a value
vars n;                     ;;; Redeclare it
n =>                        ;;; Check that the value is unchanged
** 3
```

2.10.1 Local variables in procedures

We can declare a variable to be 'local' to a procedure. When a variable is declared locally, the previous value of the variable is saved whenever the procedure is run. When a procedure which uses a local variable exits, the saved value of the variable is restored. For example:

```
define b;
    vars x;  ;;; Declare X as a local variable to the procedure B.
    2 -> x; x => ;;; Assign 2 to X and print the value of X.
enddefine;

define a;
    vars x;  ;;; Declare X as a local variable to the procedure A.
    3 -> x; x =>  ;;; Assign 3 to X and print the value of X.
    b();     ;;; Run the procedure B.
    x =>     ;;; Print the value of X again.
enddefine;
```

If we call the procedure a by typing

```
a();
```

the following values of x are printed out:

```
** 3  ;;; the value assigned to X in the procedure A
** 2  ;;; the value assigned to X in the procedure B
** 3  ;;; the restored value of X after exiting from procedure B
```

If we then ask for the value of x after a returns, by typing

```
x =>
```

we see that it has the value if had before we called a:

```
** <undef x>
```

A value of the form <undef . . .> indicates that the variable has not yet been given a value. The assignments to x inside a have not made any difference to its value outside a, since it was local to a. When the procedure finished, the saved value of x, that is, the value it had before a assigned anything to it, was restored.

If a local variable is accessed inside a procedure before it is assigned a value within that procedure, it will still have the value it had when the procedure was entered. Entering a procedure does not automatically overwrite the values of its local variables:

```
vars n;
3 -> n;

define printn();
    vars n;
    n =>              ;;; Inspect initial value of N inside PRINTN
    n+1 -> n;         ;;; Locally increment N
    n =>              ;;; Inspect new value
enddefine;

printn();
** 3                  ;;; Initial value same as before PRINTN called
** 4                  ;;; Incremented value
n =>
** 3                  ;;; Old value restored on exit
```

The fact that the initial value of a local variable is the same as the value it had before entry to the relevant procedure can sometimes be convenient.

2.10.2 Global variables in procedures

When a procedure uses a variable which is not declared locally within it, the variable is said to be 'global' with respect to the procedure. When a procedure that uses a variable globally exits, any change that the procedure has made to the value of the variable remains in force. For example, the variable x is now global to procedure b, below:

```
define b;
    2 -> x; x =>  ;;; Assign 2 to X and print the value of X
enddefine;
```

Calling the procedure a now causes the following to happen:

```
a();

** 3  ;;; the value assigned to X in procedure A
** 2  ;;; the value assigned to X in procedure B
** 2  ;;; value of X is not reset since X is global to B
```

Asking for the value of x after the procedure a has exited still produces <undef x> since x was declared as a local variable to procedure a.

POP-11 provides an alternative form of variable declaration for declaring variables local to a procedure, using lvars rather than vars. The difference is that lvars variables are 'lexically' or 'statically' scoped, whereas vars variables are dynamically scoped. All the examples in this book use vars, since for many purposes they are more flexible, though they are slightly less efficient. If you have access to POPLOG try help lvars and help efficiency for more information.

2.11 IDENTIFIERS AND VARIABLES

We have used the word 'variable' since that is common terminology. Strictly speaking there are identifiers which are words which can be used to name some - thing, and only a subset of these correspond to variables, that is, words whose values can be changed. There are also constant identifiers built into the system, for instance true, false and termin. Any attempt to assign something to one of them, or to declare them as variables, will produce a mishap message. The POP-11 word "undef" is used as a constant name of itself, to indicate something which has not yet been given a value.

Constants

The user can also declare an identifier to be a constant. This can sometimes be useful for increasing efficiency, or to prevent the value of a global identifier being changed accidentally. For example

```
constant myname;
'fred' -> myname;
```

A single assignment to a constant is allowed, but an attempt to change it will fail. For example:

```
'joe' -> myname;
```

causes the following mishap message to be printed out:

```
;;; MISHAP - ILLEGAL ASSIGNMENT TO CONSTANT
;;; INVOLVING:   myname
```

2.12 SECTIONS

Identifiers can be used on a localised basis using POP-11 sections. That is, identifiers in a portion of POP-11 program between the brackets section . . . endsection will not clash with the same identifiers used elsewhere to refer to different objects. Sections are of great value when identifiers used in system and library programs must not interfere either with identifiers declared elsewhere in the same programs, or with identifiers declared in the user's program when using such facilities.

Sections restrict access to variables in separate parts of a program. Some variables must be accessed in sections other than the ones they are declared in (or how would you ever make use of them?). For this reason you can 'import' and 'export' identifiers to and from sections. Exporting an identifier makes it available outside the section it was declared in. Importing an identifier makes it available in sections other than the one it was declared in. Declaring an identifier to be global makes it available in any section. Examples of exporting and importing identifiers follow.

Constructing sections

The syntax for constructing sections is:

```
section <pathname> <imports> => <exports>;
    <expression sequence>;
endsection;
```

<imports> and <exports> are both optional sequences of words, the => being omitted if there are no <exports>.

Suppose we declare the following variables and procedures:

```
vars list; [this is the outer list] -> list;
vars another_list; [this list gets imported] -> another_list;

define print_list(l);
    vars x;
    for x in l do spr(x); endfor;
enddefine;
```

We now declare a section, with some <imports> and <exports>:

```
section list_section another_list => addup;

define print_list( );   ;;; This version of PRINT_LIST will not
    vars x;             ;;; clash with the one outside the section
    for x in another_list  ;;; The local version can access the
    do spr(x);             ;;; imported variable ANOTHER_LIST
    endfor;
enddefine;

define addup(list) -> n; ;;; This will be available outside the
    vars x;              ;;; section, since it is exported
    0 -> n;
    for x in list do x + n -> n; endfor;
enddefine;

endsection;
```

If you declare something which you know you are going to want to import into lots of sections, you can declare it to be global:

```
global vars root_two; 1.4142 -> root_two;

define global mylistprint(list);
    vars x;
    for x in list
    do  pr(x); pr(newline);
    endfor;
enddefine;
```

After either sort of global declaration you can use the identifier inside any section. There are some fairly complex things you can do with sections, such as nesting them, or accessing the values that identifiers had inside sections from which they were not exported. We will not go into the details of these advanced uses — if you have a POPLOG system you can look in ref sections.

2.13 PROCEDURES

When we define a procedure, we are declaring an identifier whose value is to be a procedure. For example, here is the definition of a procedure called silly which takes one thing as input and then prints it out twice using the print arrow:

```
define silly(item);
    item =>  item =>
enddefine;
```

This contains an implicit declaration of silly as the name of an identifier, whose initial value is the procedure defined here. It also contains an implicit declaration of item as a local variable of the procedure.

Procedure calls

The definition of silly, above, includes two imperatives. The instructions are not obeyed when POP-11 reads in the definition. Rather, a procedure in which the instructions are stored for future use is created. So we need a way of telling POP-11 when to obey the instructions. We also need to tell POP-11 what it should treat as the item to be printed out twice. To do this we write the name of the procedure, followed by the input locals, if there are any, in parentheses. For example:

```
silly([mary had a little lamb]);

** [mary had a little lamb]
** [mary had a little lamb]
```

Terminology varies. We may say that the procedure is 'run', 'invoked', 'obeyed', 'executed', 'applied' or 'called'. These all mean roughly the same, though some may be more natural in certain contexts. For instance, we would say that the procedure silly was 'applied to' the list [mary had a little lamb] , or that it was 'run with' the argument [mary had a little lamb] .

Some procedures take no arguments. They are run without being applied to anything. One such is sysdaytime, which produces a string of information about the date and time. We can run it, with no arguments, and use the print arrow to print out the resulting string. Note the empty parentheses:

```
sysdaytime() =>
** Mon Feb 18 17:40:05 GMT 1985
```

The format of the result of this procedure may be different under different operating systems.

POP-11 will not start executing the imperative until it has read in a semi-colon or a print arrow; until then it is not sure whether the imperative is complete, or whether some additional portion is to be added. This is because POP-11 allows a single command to be spread over several lines.

Procedures which produce results

Just as procedure definitions can extend the range of imperatives in POP-11, so can they also be used to extend the range of expressions. For example, here is a procedure which, when given two numbers, produces another:

```
define doublesum(num1, num2) -> total;
    num1 + num1 + num2 + num2 -> total;
enddefine;
```

There are several different formats for procedure definitions, but we have now seen the two most common — those which produce results, and those which do not.

Given the above definition of doublesum, the expression

```
doublesum(2, 3)
```

invokes the procedure, applying it to the numbers 2 and 3. Since the procedure produces a result, namely $2 + 2 + 3 + 3 = 10$, we say that the whole expression 'denotes' the number 10. Similarly

```
doublesum(4, 5)
```

is an expression which denotes the number 18. Notice that doublesum is effectively the same procedure as perim, defined in Section 1.2, even though its name, and the names of the variables it uses, are different.

The arithmetic procedures + and * also produce results. By applying them to arguments, we can form expressions denoting numbers. For example

```
3 + 5 * 2
```

denotes 13.

When we define a procedure we specify whether it needs to be given any input and whether it produces any results. For example, the procedure silly was defined to take one thing as its input. We say it takes one 'argument'. doublesum takes two arguments, and produces one result. silly prints things out using the print arrow; that is not the same as producing a result.

When a procedure produces a result, the result is available for use by other procedures. If something is printed out on the terminal screen, it cannot be used by other procedures, since the computer cannot see what is on the screen. Results are stored in a special portion of the computer memory called the 'stack' (see Chapter 3 for more on the stack). When a result is produced it can be assigned to a variable, used as input to another procedure, or printed out:

```
vars x;
3 + 4 -> x;         ;;; assign the result of + to X.
silly(3 + 4) =>     ;;; result of + is input to SILLY.
** 7
3 + 4 =>            ;;; result of + is printed out by =>.
** 7
```

The word 'output' can be ambiguous, referring either to something printed out, or to a result left by a procedure on the stack. When we talk about a procedure producing output, the context should make clear which is intended: printing something out, or leaving a result on the stack.

2.14 CONDITIONALS AND CONDITIONS

Conditional expressions are commands to do something if some condition holds. POP-11 includes conditionals, of which a simple form would be:

```
if <condition> then <imperative> endif
```

For example, the conditional statement

```
if x = 10 then x => endif;
```

will print out the value of x if it is 10, and do nothing otherwise. Conditionals must include a 'condition' between the if and the then. Any POP-11 imperatives, or a sequence of imperatives typed over several lines, can appear after the then.

A condition is an expression which, when executed, produces a result. The imperative following the then is executed unless the result is <false>.

Predicates

Any procedure whose result is always a boolean is called a predicate. Besides = for comparing the equality of two items, there are several other built-in predicates. > and <, for example, compare two numbers and produce a boolean:

```
x > 10  =>
** <true>
```

Some predicates, for example those to recognise classes of object, take a single argument. Some are shown below:

```
isinteger(99) =>
** <true>

isword("isinteger") =>
** <true>

isprocedure(isinteger) =>
** <true>

isprocedure("isinteger") =>
** <false>
```

The last three examples here illustrate the difference between a word and its value. "isinteger" is a word, whose value is a procedure. When we test "isinteger" to see what it is, we see that it is a word. When we test isinteger, we are working on the value of this word, so we see that it is a procedure.

2.15 WORD-FORMATION RULES IN POP-11

We have assumed so far that we can treat POP-11 programs as made of numbers and words which can be combined to form expressions, or imperatives, or sequences thereof. But what is actually typed in, or read in from a file, is a sequence of characters. For instance, the following is a sequence of eight characters (a space is a character), which has to be broken up into four items, the number 3, the word +, the number 5 and the word =>:

```
3 + 5 =>
```

POP-11 applies quite complex rules to decide how to divide up the stream of characters into meaningful chunks. For instance, if you type

```
[a little list,and,6*5]
```

it is read as eleven items (including the two list brackets) and, in fact, will be interpreted as an instruction to build a list containing nine items (seven words and two numbers).

To do this, POP-11 needs rules saying which sorts of characters can be joined up with which, since you do not always have to use spaces to separate things. Besides things like spaces, tabs and newlines, which are normally ignored by POP-11, the types of characters in Table 2.1 are recognised.

Table 2.1 – POP-11 characters

Numeric	0 1 2 3 4 5 6 7 8 9
Alphabetic	a b c d e f g . . . z
	A B C D E F G . . . Z
Signs	! $ & + – : < = > ? @ ^	˝ / *
Underscore	_
Separators	; " % ( ) , . [ ] { }
String quote	'
Character quote	`

POP-11 combines a letter followed by a series of letters and numbers into a single word. However, if you start with a number, then as soon as a non-number is reached (for example the l in 1list) POP-11 assumes that it should insert a break. That is, the text is separated into a number followed by a word. This can be shown by typing in the following instructions to create and print out lists:

```
[list3] =>
** [list3]

[3list] =>
** [3 list]
```

The second list is taken to have two elements, a number and a word. The first contains a single word list3.

A numeric character can also be buried in the middle of a word which starts with letters, for example list3a. So letters stick to each other, and to numbers 'on the right', or 'embedded'.

The word quote symbol ". . ." tells POP-11 that you wish to refer to a word rather than the value associated with a word. For example:

```
"list3" =>
** list3
```

If you type an illegal combination of characters in word quotes, you will get a mishap message:

```
"3list" =>
;;; MISHAP: IQW INCORRECT QUOTED WORD
;;; INVOLVING: 3
```

You can also make a word out of certain non-alpha-numeric characters, the sign characters:

```
"*+*+*::\^" =>

** *+*+*::\^
```

You cannot mix letters and sign characters:

```
"+x" =>
;;; MISHAP - MEI: MISPLACED EXPRESSION ITEM
;;; INVOLVING:  FOUND x READING TO "
;;; DOING    :  " compile
```

In a list they will be separated into two words:

```
[+x] =>
** [+ x]
```

The underscore character can be used to join alpha-numeric characters to sign characters. A list containing one word follows:

```
[+_x] =>
** [+_x]
```

The underscore can also be used as a convenient way of producing long names which are readable. For example, the following is the name of a system variable:

```
pop_readline_prompt
```

In general, a sequence of characters made of sign characters and letters will be broken at the point where the two sorts of characters meet, unless they are joined by an underscore. Other examples of simple words are:

```
fast_++           ++_lists_++
```

Two of the sign characters, / and *, play a special role in that they can be combined to form the comment brackets, explained above. So /* and */ cannot be used as words.

The separator characters cannot be used to join up with anything else, except for the use of . in decimal numbers, for example **66.35**, and of : for changing the base of a number. This is because they have special roles in the syntax of POP-11 as we shall see later.

The semicolon, though normally a separator which marks the end of an imperative, has a special role if repeated three times without anything in between. It marks a comment, as explained above.

2.16 STRINGS

Strings, created using the string quote characters, can contain any sequence of arbitrary character, as in:

```
'this is a *+*+*+* string %&$%$ of rubbish!!!!'
```

If you wish to include the string quote itself in a string, it must be preceded by \ to indicate that it does not mark the end of the string. Here is a string containing the string quote:

```
'isn\'t it' =>
** isn't it
```

The \ must also be used if you want to produce a string which extends over several lines, as in:

```
'This is a string which\
extends over two lines' =>

** This is a string which
extends over two lines
```

Note that strings are normally printed without the outer quotes, unless true is assigned to pop_pr_quotes.

Strings are not words. They do not have values, and cannot operate as identifiers. They are just structures containing sequences of characters. See Section 10.2 for more on strings.

2.17 CHARACTER CODES

Characters themselves are represented by integers less than 128. Since it is difficult to remember which number represents which character (the so-called 'ASCII code'), the character quote `can be used to tell POP-11 to read a character as representing the number. For example:

```
`A` =>
** 65

`5` =>
** 53
```

We see from this example that the character code for A is 65, and for 5 it is 53.

Exercises
1. What do expressions refer to?
2. What do imperatives refer to?
3. Give examples of some of the sorts of objects POP-11 expressions can refer to.
4. Give examples of some of the sorts of imperatives one can construct in POP-11 and explain what they do.
5. Define a procedure which takes in three numbers, adds up the first two, and then multiplies the result by the third. Your definition could start:

```
define addmult(x, y, z) -> result;
```

6. What is the difference between defining a procedure and calling, or invoking, it?

7. Explain, with examples, what it means to say that a procedure takes a certain number of arguments, and does or does not produce a result.

8. What is the difference between => and ==>?

9. What is a comment, and how are comments expressed in POP-11?

10. What will the following print:

    pr(99);spr(100);pr(101);spr(102);pr(103);

11. What are predicates and how are they used in conditions?

12. Which of the following words are legal in POP-11?

    i. "cat5"; ii. "5cat"; iii. "**+**"; iv. "*cat*";

    v. "_5cat"; vi "*_cat"

2.18 BUILT-IN POP-11 DATA TYPES

We have seen that POP-11 allows you to construct expressions which denote objects, and we have seen some examples of these expressions. Programming languages differ in the range of types of objects they can refer to. Often there is a fixed set of data types built into the language, for example numbers, words and lists.

Some languages, including POP-11, allow you to extend the set of data types indefinitely. In POP-11 this requires using the procedure conskey, or the recordclass and vectorclass declarations explained in Section 10.3. Table 2.2 summarises the built-in data types introduced so far. Table 2.3 shows additional POP-11 data types encountered in later chapters.

Table 2.2 – Basic built-in POP-11 data types

Words	"cat", "dog", "***", "a", "xxx_yyy", "(", "!+*+*+!"
Strings	'a', '21385d73::;+*)(&%', 'string with spaces'

Words, unlike strings, are stored in a dictionary, and may be used in a program to refer to something else, for example, they can be used as variable names. Expressions denoting words have strict formation rules, sketched above, and cannot contain spaces, as strings can. (However, there are procedures which can construct words with arbitrary combinations of characters, even though they cannot be typed in directly.)

Numbers There are two sorts of numbers:

    Integers: 66 −33 99999

    Decimals: 66.0 −33.0 77.35 9999.532 −6666.0

Numbers may also be represented relative to a base. The base is indicated by an integer followed by a colon preceding the number itself. Thus, binary numbers are represented with the prefix 2:.

    2:100 is the same as 4

    2:1011 is the same as 11

    8:101 is the same as 65

2:1.1   is the same as 1.5

8:1.1   is the same as 1.125

Bases up to 36 may be specified. For bases greater than 10, the letters A–Z may be used as 'numerals'. For instance, 16:1B denotes 27 (once times 16, plus B times 1, where B stands for 11). The prefix 10: is redundant. 10:999 = 999.

Characters `a`, `B`, `9`, `(`

These are represented using the character quote symbol . In the computer they are represented as integers in the range 0 to 127. For example `A` is 65, `B` is 66, `a` is 97.

Warning: `a` is a character, whereas 'a' is a string.

Booleans (or truth-values)

There are only two of these – <true> and <false>.

Lists

These may be used to form a single object composed of arbitrarily many objects of any type, including lists. Many examples of lists are given in this book. Lists are, strictly speaking, a 'derived' data type in POP-11 because they are constructed out of the data type 'pair'.

Procedures

These are sets of instructions, which tell the computer to do something. Some are built into the POP-11 system. Others are added by the user. Unlike some languages, POP-11 treats procedures as objects, just like numbers or words. For example, procedures can be stored in lists, or assigned to variables.

Undefs

When a new variable is created, it is given a default value, which is a special object which will print out something like <undef xx>. Meeting one of these in an error message is usually an indication that you have forgotten to initialise a variable with an appropriate value.

Termin

termin is a unique object used to indicate the end of a sequence of items, for example, the end of a sequence of characters read from a file.

Table 2.3 – Additional built-in POP-11 data types

Pairs

These are two-element structures used to build lists. For example, the list [a b c] is represented by a pair whose first element is the word a. The second element of this pair is another pair. This pair contains b as its first element, and yet another pair as its second. This third pair contains c as its first element, and the empty list nil as its second to mark the end of the chain. Most of the time users do not need to think about pairs. The facilities for building and manipulating lists, described later, are designed to hide such irrelevant details!

Arrays

These are n-dimensional structures whose components are accessed by a collection of n numbers, where n can be 1 or more. For example, a two-dimensional array might represent a picture, and its components could be accessed by giving two numbers representing distance along and distance up.

Vectors: {a b c}{cat mouse 3 4}{'a string' in a vector}

These are like lists, but stored more compactly in the computer. They are sometimes less convenient to use

Closures

A closure is a combination of a procedure and some data for it to operate on.

Processes

A process is a combination of a procedure, some data and a record of how far the procedure has got in its execution. The process can be suspended and resumed as required.

Keys

Each data type has associated with it an object known as a key which is a structure containing information about all objects of that type, such as what they are called, how they are to be printed, and how many elements they are made of.

Properties

A property is a table of associations between objects. A property can function as a sort of memory of what is linked with what.

Devices

These are records associated with files, terminals and other means of communication between the POP-11 system and the rest of the world.

We will return to these additional structures in later chapters.

There is a portion of the computer memory which is referred to as the 'stack'. This is used as a general 'communication area' by POP-11. We shall often refer to it as if it were an object though, strictly speaking, it is not. It cannot be manipulated like an object. For example, objects can be put on the stack, but the stack cannot be put on the stack. The next chapter elaborates.

3

The stack

The 'user stack', usually abbreviated to the 'stack', is a portion of memory that POP-11 uses for temporarily storing information needed by procedures when they interact.

It is called a stack because, like a stack of plates, you can add things to, and take things off, the top. The thing you take off will always be the last thing that was put on. Procedures in POP-11 get their arguments from the stack, and leave their results on the stack. They interact with other procedures via the stack. For example, if procedure a wants to run procedure b giving it certain input arguments, it puts the arguments on the stack and then just runs b; b takes the arguments off the stack as needed. If, when b has finished, it has any information for a, it leaves it on the stack so that a can take it off as needed.

A full understanding of POP-11 requires an understanding of the stack. What follows is an introductory explanation.

3.1 ASSIGNMENT AND THE STACK

The assignment arrow, $\rightarrow$, removes an item from the top of the stack and stores it somewhere else, usually in a variable.

Non-destructive assignment and the stack

The normal assignment arrow removes the top item from the stack. Sometimes it is convenient to assign this top item somewhere without also removing it. Using the non-destructive assignment arrow, $\rightarrow\!\!>$, achieves this. For instance, we can assign the same thing to several different variables by doing:

```
0 ->> x -> y;
```

This puts 0 on the top of the stack, and then copies it into the variables x and y. So:

```
x =>
** 0

y =>
** 0
```

0 was removed from the top of the stack by the last assignment, which was an ordinary one.

Multiple assignments
All the following imperatives use the stack:

(i) <expression> =>
(ii) <expression>;
(iii) <expression> -> variable;
(iv) -> variable;

We can replace <expression> by a sequence of <expression>s separated by commas, and we can replace -> variable by a sequence of such things, for example:

```
1, 2, 3 -> z -> y -> x;
```

After this imperative is run, z has the value 3, y the value 2, and x the value 1.

Swapping items on the stack
Typing

```
x, y -> x -> y;
```

causes the values of x and y to be swapped. Notice that -> x removes the top item from the stack, and assigns it to x, whereas the operation

```
x;
```

just copies the value of x onto the stack, leaving x unchanged. We demonstrate this difference below:

```
vars x;
77, 88, 99;      ;;; put three things on the stack
-> x;            ;;; take one off and make it the value of X
=>
** 77 88         ;;; two things left

x; x; x; =>      ;;; copy value of X three times onto stack
** 99 99 99
```

The statement

```
-> x -> y; x, y;
```

has a rather different meaning. Effectively, it swaps the top two elements of the stack and, as a side-effect, stores the top two items in x and y. A mishap message will be printed if there are not at least two items on the stack to start with.

If we wanted to swap the first (that is, the top) and third elements of the stack we could do:

```
-> x -> y -> z; x, y, z;
```

Beware of writing programs which leave things lying around on the stack for later use in a wanton fashion. It can make programs hard to understand, debug, or modify.

3.2 ASSIGNING INTO STRUCTURES: UPDATERS AND VALOF

Besides storing things in variables, assignment can be used to store something in a structure. For example, we may create a list, then use assignment to alter its fourth element:

```
vars list; [a b c d e] -> list; list =>
** [a b c d e]

"D" -> list(4);    ;;; alter the 4th element
list =>
** [a b c D e]
```

Many procedures which are used for accessing components of data structures, for example hd and tl, have 'updaters' which can be used for assigning into their arguments. For example:

```
hd(list) =>
** a
26 -> hd(list); list =>
[26 b c D e]
```

The effect of tl's updater is a little surprising at first sight. Remember that tl gets you the remainder of a list, not the second element. So assigning to the tail of a list should change its remainder, not just its second element:

```
[a b c d] -> list;
list =>
** [a b c d]
[e f] -> tl(list); list =>
** [a e f]
```

[e f] has become the tail of list. The tail is the remainder of the list after the first element. So list is now [a e f] — the old head followed by the new tail. The old tail is lost.

Updaters are quite important in POP-11. They are procedures which insert items into structures, rather than retrieve them. The assignment arrow 'knows' that if it finds a call of a procedure to its right, the updater of the procedure is what is really wanted. A procedure call to the left of the assignment arrow will access the relevant component of the input data structure; one to its right will make whatever is on the left the contents of that component. We will see a number of other procedures with updaters in Chapter 10, and we will see how to associate an updater with a procedure in Section 11.2. We will have a look at one particularly important procedure which has an updater here, namely valof.

We have pointed out the distinction between using a word as a variable, and using it as itself. We have emphasised that if you type a word between word quotes, as in "x1", it will be used as itself, that is, as a place where the characters x and 1 are kept; whereas if you type it without the quotes, x1, it will be taken as the name of a variable. The procedure valof provides the connection between the two. valof allows you to access the value of a quoted word (or, using valof's updater, to assign to it). Assigning to a variable, and using valof to update the value of a quoted word, are absolutely equivalent. Accessing a variable, and using valof to access the value of a quoted word, are absolutely equivalent.

Examples:

```
vars x; 1 -> x;          ;;; Declare X, give it an initial value
valof("x") =>            ;;; Access that value via VALOF
** 1
3 -> valof("x");         ;;; Update the value via VALOF
x =>                     ;;; Access it using X as a variable
** 3
valof(x) =>              ;;; Using VALOF on X, rather than "X",
;;; MISHAP - WORD NEEDED  ;;; is a mistake. We are effectively
;;; INVOLVING:  3        ;;; trying to "dereference" X twice
;;; DOING    :  valof compile
```

Exercise

1. Suppose we set "y" to be the value of x, and [a b c] to be the value of y:

    ```
    "y" -> x;
    [a b c] -> y;
    ```

    What will the following do?

    ```
    (i)     y =>
    (ii)    valof("y") =>
    (iii)   valof(x) =>
    (iv)    valof("x") =>
    ```

3.3 PROCEDURES AND THE STACK

We now define a procedure to illustrate how procedures use the stack. sumsq, below, takes two numbers and produces the sum of their squares as its result:

```
define sumsq(x, y) -> r;
    (x * x) + (y * y) -> r;
enddefine;
```

sumsq has three local variables, called x, y and r. When it runs, there must be at least two items on the user stack. (There may be more than two if other procedures have stored information which is to be used later.)

The top two items are removed from the stack. The top one is assigned to y, and the next one to x. (Note their order of appearance in the procedure heading.) When the procedure finishes, the value of the variable r, whatever it is, is left on the stack. Running sumsq, by doing something like

```
vars z; sumsq(3, 4) -> z;
```

translates into the following:

(i) Put 3 on the stack.
(ii) Put 4 on the stack.
(iii) Run the procedure sumsq, which takes two things off the stack, and when it finishes puts one thing back on it.
(iv) Remove the top item from the stack and store it in the variable z.

3.4 MISHAPS AND THE STACK

There is a very common mishap message associated with the stack, namely:

```
MISHAP - STACK EMPTY (missing argument? missing result?)
```

STACK EMPTY mishaps happen when a procedure, or the assignment arrow, tries to take something off the stack when there is nothing there. For example, the command

```
sumsq(3) -> z;    ;;; put 3 on the stack and then run SUMSQ
```

produces the mishap:

```
;;; MISHAP - STE: STACK EMPTY (missing argument? missing result?)
;;; DOING    :  sumsq compile nextitem compile
```

sumsq takes whatever is on the top of the stack (in this case 3) and assigns it to y. Then it tries to assign the item on the top of the stack to x and finds nothing left. This situation causes the mishap message. Note that the DOING line of the mishap message tells you that sumsq was running at the time that the stack was found to be empty.

We can also have a procedure which fails to produce a result. For example:

```
define sumsq(x, y);
    (x * x) + (y * y) -> x;
enddefine;
```

Typing

```
sumsq(3, 4);
```

gives x and y the values 3 and 4 respectively. sumsq assigns the result of the expression

```
(x * x) + (y * y)
```

locally to x. At this stage, nothing is left on the stack. Moreover, the heading of the definition does not specify that x is an output local variable for sumsq, so the value of x is not left on the stack. Nor is anything else left on the stack, as is shown by doing:

```
sumsq(3, 4) =>
**
```

If we type

```
sumsq(3, 4) -> z;
```

we get the mishap message:

```
;;; MISHAP - STE: STACK EMPTY (missing argument? missing result?)
;;; DOING    : compile nextitem compile
```

This time sumsq is run but finishes up with nothing on the stack. The assignment arrow, however, tries to take something off the stack to give to z, and at this point finds the stack empty. A mishap message results. The problem is the missing result from sumsq. The DOING line of the mishap message does not mention sumsq because sumsq has finished running and is no longer active when the error is detected. It is sometimes difficult to track down errors caused by a procedure failing to return a result. Usually you can get clues by looking at which procedures were active at the time.

3.5 CONDITIONALS AND THE STACK

Previously we noticed that the use of a conditional like

```
if x = 10 then x => endif;
```

depended on the fact that = is a predicate, that is, a procedure producing a boolean result which is left on the stack. You can think of a conditional imperative of the form

```
if <condition> then <action> endif
```

as being roughly equivalent to this:

(i) Put the value of the <condition> on the stack.
(ii) If the top element of the stack is not <false>, perform the <action>, otherwise jump to after the endif.

This means that if the expression between if and then produces no result, then an error will occur. For example, 3 = x produces a boolean result, but the assignment 3 -> x does not, so:

```
if 3 -> x then x => endif;

;;; MISHAP - STE: STACK EMPTY (missing argument? missing result?)
```

Since POP-11 treats anything other than <false> as <true> in a condition, it is sometimes convenient to define a procedure which returns either <false>, or some object that it discovers. For example, findword, below, searches down a list looking for any word; instead of returning <true> if it finds one, it returns the word itself. If there are no words, it returns <false>:

```
define findword(list) -> result;
    vars item;
    for item in list do
        if isword(item) then    ;;; if a word is found,
            item -> result;      ;;; make it the result of FINDWORD
            return();            ;;; and leave this procedure
        endif;
    endfor;
    false -> result;            ;;; otherwise return <false>
enddefine;
```

To test findword, do:

```
findword([1 2 3 4 5 6]) =>
** <false>

findword([1 2 3 4 five 6]) =>
** five
```

findword might be used in a conditional expression with the non-destructive assignment arrow thus:

```
vars w;
if findword(list) ->> w then
    ... do something with w ...;
    else report_failure();
endif;
```

The following use of a boolean expression using the non-destructive assignment arrow is extremely common:

```
vars x;
until   (itemread() ->> x) == termin do
    ... do something with x ...;
enduntil;
```

Here we are using the procedure itemread, which reads items from the terminal. Each time we read an item, we assign it as the value of x, so that we can make use of it later; and we also compare it with the distinguished item termin, which will be returned when we have finished reading items. This format allows us to specify loops in which the 'step' is performed before the test.

Exercise

2.   Work out and write down what happens when the following imperative is
run:

```
(((2 + 3) * 4) + 5) - 2 =>
```


3.6   STACK MANIPULATING PROCEDURES

POP-11 provides built-in procedures for manipulating the stack. The most
common ones follow:

stacklength

This procedure can be used to find out how many things are on the stack. When
invoked it counts the number of items on the stack and then leaves that number
on top of the stack, for example:

```
2 + 3, 9 - 5, stacklength() =>
** 5 4 2
```

stacklength is called. Everything on the stack is counted. Expressions are evaluated. stacklength counts two items, 5 (from the expression 2 + 3) and 4 (from
the expression 9 − 5). The print arrow removes the items and the result of
stacklength from the stack, and prints the values out.

erase

The procedure erase removes one item from the stack, for example:

```
2 + 3, 9 - 5, erase() =>
** 5
```

and

```
5 + 5, 66, erase(), 8 * 8, 10 - 5, erase() =>
** 10 64
```

The assignment arrow followed by ; or , (or any other expression terminator)
has the same effect as erase( ). Thus:

```
5 + 5, 66, ->, 8 * 8, 10 - 5, -> =>
** 10 64
```

Whether you use this or erase is a matter of taste. However, erase has to be used
when a stack-clearing procedure is referred to explicitly, for example passed to
another procedure as input.

   erase is used if you want only one of the results of a procedure which
produces two results. For example, the operation // performs integer division
putting the remainder and the quotient on the stack:

```
23 // 6 =>
** 5 3
```

To assign only the remainder to x, you could do:

```
erase(23 // 6) -> x;
x =>
** 5
```

or

```
23 // 6 -> -> x;
x =>
** 5
```

To assign the divisor, first assign the top of the stack, then erase the second result:

```
erase(23 // 6 -> x);
x =>
** 3
```

or

```
23 // 6 -> x -> ;
x =>
** 3
```

erasenum

The procedure erasenum takes an integer and removes that number of items from the stack. For example:

```
1, 2, 3, 4, 5, 6; erasenum(2) =>
** 1 2 3 4
```

The above could also be expressed, perhaps rather confusingly, as:

```
erasenum(1, 2, 3, 4, 5, 6, 2) =>
```

clearstack

This procedure removes everything from the stack. For example:

```
1, 2, 3, 4 =>
** 1 2 3 4

1, 2, 3, 4; clearstack() =>
**
```

subscr_stack

This procedure takes a number as input, and returns or updates the corresponding item on the stack. It allows the stack to be used as if it were an array. For example, to update the stack we could do:

```
1, 2, 3, 4, 5;              ;;; put 1, 2, 3, 4, 5 on the stack
10 -> subscr_stack(3); => ;;; replace third item on stack with 10
** 1 2 10 4 5              ;;; print out the contents of the stack
```

To return the fifth item we could do:

```
1, 2, 3, 4, 5; subscr_stack(5) =>
** 1 2 3 4 5 1
```

If there are not at least n items on the stack, an error will occur.

These stack manipulating procedures should be used with care. They can sometimes be used to produce elegant solutions to problems. They can also be used to write programs which are incomprehensible, which are impossible to debug, and whose effects are thoroughly unpredictable.

Exercises

3. What will be printed out by the following?

```
i. 1, 2, 3, 4;        ii. 1, 2, 3, 4;
   -> x;                 ->> x;
   =>                    =>
   x =>                  x =>
```

4. If you type 1, 2, 3, 4;
   (i) What is on the top of the stack?
   (ii) In what order will => print out the stack?
   (iii) If a procedure of one argument is run, what will its argument be?

5. What does the following imperative print?

```
6, 7, 9 - 5, ->, 4 + 2, 10, 3, -> =>
```

6. The imperative
   ```
   18 // 4 =>
   ```
   puts 2 and 4 on the stack and then prints them ** 2 4. Using **erase**, how could you get just the remainder printed out (that is, erase the divisor from the stack)?

4

Arithmetic

4.1 ARITHMETIC: BASIC FACILITIES

POP-11 has two sorts of numbers – integers and decimals. Decimal numbers
are divided into single decimals and double decimals, with double decimals
providing more precision than single decimals. Decimal numbers are often called
'reals', or 'floating point numbers'. This is because their accuracy is measured
in terms of the number of significant digits rather than absolute value. 'Floating
point' is a more accurate term than 'decimal' – it is possible in POP-11 to change
the base which we are using for our numbers, so there could be binary floating
point numbers, or octal floating point numbers. We ignore this technicality
most of the time, using 'floating point' and 'decimal' almost interchangeably
except in contexts where it would lead to real ambiguity or confusion.

There are several procedures for manipulating numbers. We have seen a
number of the more basic ones already. This section simply provides a summary.
Most of these have names which are infix operators. That is, they can be used
to create expressions without using parentheses, for example 3 + 5 and 77 * 9,
although it is legal to write + (3, 5) or * (77, 9) instead if you prefer.

Table 4.1 shows the operations that are available for constructing arithmetic
expressions.

Most of the operations in Table 4.1 are 'binary' operations. That is, they
require two arguments. For example, the expression

    3 + 4

applies the operation + to the two arguments 3 and 4. It denotes the number 7.
The arguments may themselves be complex expressions, for example:

    (3 + 4) + (5 + 6)

Table 4.1 — Operations for constructing arithmetic expressions

---

+	add two numbers
—	subtract two numbers, or negate one number
*	multiply two numbers
**	exponentiation: for example a ** 3 means a*a*a, that is, a cubed
/	divide first number by second
//	divide first number by second, produce remainder and quotient

>	test two numbers: <true> if first greater than second
<	test two numbers: <true> if first less than second
>=	test two numbers: <true> if first greater than or equal to second
<=	test two numbers: <true> if first less than or equal to second

x div y   returns the number of times y goes into x. Both integers
x rem y   returns the remainder on dividing x by y
   (Instead of rem it is possible to use mod.)

The operation — can be binary (two arguments) or unary (one argument). POP-11 works out from the context which it is. When it is unary, as in

    - 4

or

    - (3 + 5)

it produces a number by negating its argument. When it is a binary operator, as in

    3 - 4

or

    (2 + 1) - (2 + 2)

it subtracts the second argument from the first. So the latter expression denotes the number —1.

In general, the sort of thing denoted by an expression involving a particular operator depends on the operator. Consider:

    99 > (X + Y)

This takes the number 99, and the number denoted by the expression (x + y), and puts <true> or <false> onto the stack, depending on whether the first number is greater than or less than the second. That is, > is a binary operator, taking two numbers and producing a boolean as a result. So:

    99 > 66 =>   66 > 99 =>
    ** <true>   ** <false>

4.2 OTHER ARITHMETIC PROCEDURES

Table 4.2 summarises the remainder of the built-in POP-11 procedures for constructing arithmetic expressions.

Table 4.2 — Procedures for constructing arithmetic expressions

abs(x)	absolute value (modulus) of x
fracof(x)	fractional part of a decimal number
intof(x)	integer part of a decimal number, positive or negative
max(x,y)	the bigger of two numbers
min(x,y)	the smaller of two numbers
sign(x)	−1 if x is negative, +1 if positive, 0 if x = 0, or 0.0
random(x)	a random integer in range 1 to x
round(x)	the integer nearest to x
sin(x)	trigonometric sine of angle
cos(x)	trigonometric cosine of angle
arcsin(x)	arc sin of angle — inverse of sin
tan(x)	trigonometric tangent of angle
arccos(x)	trigonometric arc cosine of angle — inverse of cos
arctan(x)	trigonometric arc tangent of angle — inverse of tan
exp(x)	exponential of x (e to the power x)
log(x)	natural logarithm of a number — inverse of exp
negate(x)	negation of the number (that is, − x)
sqrt(x)	square root of number

You may be surprised to see negate. This procedure is useful when unary minus is required as an argument to, or result of, a procedure. Note also that the trigonometric procedures use degrees, unless the variable popradians is set to <true>. The default is <false>, that is, use degrees. (This is one of a large collection of user definable global variables controlling the behaviour of POP-11. See help popvars.)

All of these procedure names can be used to create expressions denoting numbers. Thus sqrt(9) denotes the number 3.0, and max(4,77) denotes the number 77.

Arithmetic expressions can be embedded in others. For example, the expression

```
tan(23 + 22)
```

is equivalent to:

```
tan(45)
```

They both denote the number 1.0 (if popradians is <false>).

```
tan(45) + tan(45)
```

denotes the number 2.0.

```
max(min(66,33), min(999,9))
```

denotes the number 33, as does:

```
max(min(66-5, 33), min(999, 9+9))
```

4.3 READING AND WRITING NUMBERS

Programs that are to use numbers have to be able to read them in and write them out. Most of the time the standard POP-11 procedures for reading and writing things will do what you want. Sometimes you want to have explicit control over how it is done. You might, for instance, want to be able to type in numbers using a base other than 10 (e.g. binary numbers), you might want them printed using a different base, or you might want to control how many of the digits in a floating point number get printed.

Inputting numbers with a radix other than 10

POP-11 will read in binary numbers if they are preceded by '2:', e.g.

```
2:111 =>
** 7
```

Similarly, octal numbers may be preceded by 8:

```
8:111 =>
** 73
```

Floating point numbers may also be input relative to a non-standard base, for example:

```
2:11.11 =>
** 3.75
```

Any number from 2 to 36 may be used as a base. If the base is greater than 10, the letters A–Z (uppercase only) can be used in the number to represent digit values from 10 to 35. For example, 16:1FFA represents 8186 as a hexadecimal number.

pop_pr_radix

The variable pop_pr_radix controls the base to which numbers are printed out. It is user assignable and defaults to 10. By making it 16, numbers can be printed in hexadecimal, for example:

```
16 -> pop_pr_radix;
16 =>
** 10
15 =>
** F
```

The printing of floating point numbers is also controlled by pop_pr_radix:

```
16 -> pop_pr_radix;
15.55 =>
** F.8CCCCD
```

popdprecision

In POP-11, the first six digits of a decimal number (excluding leading zeros) are significant no matter where the decimal point is. For example, the command

```
sqrt(2) =>
** 1.41421
```

prints six digits.

In general, numbers are read as double decimal numbers (accurate to more significant figures) but results of computations will be single decimal numbers. We illustrate this difference using the procedure dataword. When applied to an object, dataword returns its data type. For example:

```
dataword(2.25) =>    ;;; just a number
** ddecimal

vars x; 2.25 -> x;
dataword(x + 1) =>  ;;; a numerical calculation
** decimal
```

If you assign true to the variable popdprecision, the results of arithmetic procedures are left as double decimals. The default value of popdprecision is <false>. If we do

```
true -> popdprecision;
```

and ask for the square root of 2, it now prints to six fractional places:

```
sqrt(2) =>
** 1.414214
```

pop_pr_places

The variable pop_pr_places specifies the number of significant digits of a floating point number which are to be printed. It is user assignable. The default value is 6. To print the square roots of numbers to ten decimal places, we would do:

```
true -> popdprecision;
10 -> pop_pr_places;

sqrt(2) =>
** 1.4142135624
```

Assigning 0 to pop_pr_places causes floating point numbers to be printed as integers.

pop_pr_exponent

If you assign true to pop_pr_exponent (its default value is <false>) POP-11 uses exponent form for printing. For example:

```
true -> pop_pr_exponent;
sqrt(20000) =>
** 1.41421e+2
```

This notation can also be used for reading in decimals (even if true has not been assigned to pop_pr_exponent):

```
false -> pop_pr_exponent;
1.41421e+2 =>
** 141.421
```

popradians

The variable popradians controls whether the trigonometric procedures take arguments, or produce results, in degrees or radians. We can use the fact that 'pi' is a built-in constant, thus:

```
true -> popradians;
sin(90) =>
** 0.893997

sin(pi/2) =>
** 1.0

arcsin(1) =>
** 1.5708

false -> popradians;
sin(90) =>
** 1.0

sin(pi/2) =>
** 0.027412

arcsin(1) =>
** 90.0
```

4.4 RANDOM NUMBERS

POP-11 has a built-in pseudo-random number generator, namely the procedure random. random draws from a range of whole numbers determined by the size of the number given as input. That is, random(10) will always return a number lying between 1 and 10 (inclusive); random(100) between 1 and 100 inclusive, and so on. Expressions using random denote relatively unpredictable things:

```
random(10) =>
** 8
random(10) =>
** 4
random(10) =>
** 1
```

This behaviour is controlled by a variable called ranseed, whose value changes each time random is used. To make random produce a repeatable sequence of results do:

```
1 -> ranseed;
random(100) =>
** 25
random(100) =>
** 54
random(100) =>
** 4

1 -> ranseed;          ;;; restart the sequence
random(100)=>
** 25
random(100)=>
** 54
random(100)=>
** 4
```

Random decimal numbers

To produce random decimal numbers between 0 and 1, you can define the following procedure, using the fact that 536870911 is the largest integer which POP-11 can represent on 32-bit computers:

```
define random_decimal() -> result;
    (random(536870911) - 1) / 536870910 -> result
enddefine;

repeat 5 times random_decimal() => endrepeat;
** 0.078072
** 0.132751
** 0.195248
** 0.261654
** 0.328064
```

1 has to be subtracted from the result of random because random returns a result greater than, or equal to, 1. Without subtracting 1 we could never get a result of 0 from random_decimal.

Exercises

1. What are the data types of each of the following?
    (i) 33
    (ii) 33.0
    (iii) "cat"
    (iv) 'asdf;lkj876 *+*++ '
    (v) [1 2 3 4]
2. What do the following expressions denote?
    (i) 33 + 3
    (ii) 3 + (4 * 5)
    (iii) (3 + 4) * 5
    (iv) 6 - 3.0
    (v) sign(random(20))
3. What is the function of the variable popradians?
4. How can you make POP-11 print in hexadecimal form?

5. Define a procedure called new_random which produces a random number between −1 and 1.

4.5 PRECEDENCE AND PARENTHESES

This section concerns a syntactic complication in POP-11 (and most other programming languages), which we have so far illustrated without commenting on. It may seem odd to discuss a syntactic matter in a chapter on arithmetic, but it is a complication which is particularly important for arithmetic expressions.

Some procedures are run by writing their names before the parentheses, with input arguments in between parentheses, as in the imperative:

```
member(x, list) =>
```

By contrast, some other procedures, such as the arithmetic procedures +, *, and −, are invoked by writing the name in between the inputs, as in:

$$3 * 5, 77 + 7, 36 - 7$$

These infix operators are names of ordinary procedures, but have special syntactic properties to simplify their use. If the same expression contains two such infix operators, there may be an ambiguity. For example, how is $3 + 4 * 5$ to be understood? One way is to use parentheses to indicate whether the addition or the multiplication is to be done first:

```
(3 + 4) * 5 =>
** 35

3 + (4 * 5) =>
** 23
```

Parentheses are also the principal way that we get round POP-11's requirement that everything be written 'linearly'. So the 'ordinary' way of writing a division

$$\frac{7.50 + 19.43}{27}$$

becomes

```
(7.50 + 19.43)/27 =>
**   0.99740741
```

If you do not want to use brackets to disambiguate expressions, you have to make use of the 'precedence' associated with each infix operator in POP-11. A precedence is a number which determines the order in which the operations are applied. The lower the precedence, the earlier the operator is applied. Both + and − have a precedence of 5. *, /, and //, however, have a precedence of 4, indicating that these operations are applied before addition and subtraction in cases where brackets are not used to remove any ambiguity. Thus:

```
3 + 4 * 5 =>
** 23
```

Here the multiplication is done first because its precedence is lower than that of +. In the case of operators of equal precedence they are applied from left to right. For example, since * and / have equal precedence,

```
6 / 2 * 5 =>
```

is equivalent to

```
(6 / 2) * 5 =>
** 15
```

not to:

```
6 / (2 * 5) =>
** 0.6
```

Similarly,

```
3 / 4 / 5
```

is equivalent to (3 / 4) / 5 which denotes 0.15, unlike

```
3 / (4 / 5)
```

which denotes 3.75.

It is possible for an infix operation to have a negative precedence, in which case it will associate to the right, altering the order of execution − see the example in the next section.

Table 4.3 summarises the precedence for arithmetic operations.

Table 4.3 − The precedence for arithmetic operations

Operation	Precedence
div	2
rem (or mod)	2
**	3
* / //	4
+ −	5
> < >= <=	6
=	7

Using this table it can be seen that the result of typing the statement

```
3 - 2.5  ** 2 * 1.5 / 3 =>
```

will be:

```
** −0.125
```

The order of evaluation is as follows:

Original expression:	$3 - 2.5 ** 2 * 1.5 / 3$
Apply operations of precedence 3:	$3 - 6.25 * 1.5 / 3$
Apply operations of precedence 4:	$3 - 3.125$
Apply operations of precedence 5:	-0.125

The precedence associated with each operation defines an order of evaluation of an expression. If another order is required, parentheses can be used in the conventional way. For example:

```
(3 - 2.5) ** 2 * 1.5 / 3 =>
** 0.125
```

The rules of precedence apply to each expression within a pair of parentheses.

Parentheses may be nested to any depth, the expressions within inner parentheses being evaluated first.

The procedure identprops can be used to find out the precedence of an operator. For an ordinary variable the precedence is 0. For an infix operator it will be some other number. For a syntax word or macro (see Section 13.2) identprops produces the word "syntax" or "macro". If applied to a word which has not been declared by the user or the system, it produces the result "undef". If it is applied to anything other than a word a mishap message is printed. Thus:

```
identprops("+") =>
** 5

identprops(">") =>
** 6

identprops("if") =>
** syntax

identprops("help") =>
** macro

vars x; identprops("x") =>
** 0

identprops("xxx") =>
** undef
```

Defining new infix operators

Users may define their own new infix operators by specifying the precedence after the word define. Below we define an operation, ///, of precedence -3.5. It divides its first argument by the square of its second. Because /// has a negative precedence, it associates to the right:

```
define -3.5 x /// y;
    x / (y * y)
enddefine;
```

```
3 /// 4 =>
** 0.1875

4 /// 5 =>
** 0.16

3 /// 4 /// 5 =>
** 117.187

(3 /// 4) /// 5 =>
** 0.0075
```

Infix procedures are available for other purposes besides numerical operations. We shall see later that $<>$ is an infix operation which can join two objects together, and that the procedure **matches** is an infix operation used for comparing two lists. The equality symbol $=$ is also used for an infix operation.

4.6 TESTING FOR EQUALITY AND INEQUALITY

It is often necessary to use conditional imperatives in order to write flexible programs which do not always do the same thing. This requires the ability to test certain conditions to see if they are $<$true$>$ or $<$false$>$. An important class of such tests is testing for equality or similarity using the infix operators $==$ and $=$.

The infix operator $==$ tests any two objects. It returns $<$true$>$ if they are identical. 'Identical' here means not really two objects which look similar, but one and the same object. This is strict equality.

The infix operator $=$ also tests any two objects. It returns $<$true$>$ if they are identical, or if they are of the same type with the same elements, that is, if they are similar. To illustrate

```
3 == 3
```

is $<$true$>$ because it is the same thing, the number 3, that is referred to on both sides.

```
3 == 5 - 2
```

is also $<$true$>$, for the same reason.

```
[A B C] == [A B C]
```

is $<$false$>$, since there are two different lists. Each time POP-11 reads in [. . .] it creates a new list, even if there was a similar one earlier.

```
[A B C] = [A B C]
```

is $<$true$>$ since there are two similar lists, that is, each of their elements are $=$.

```
'a string' == 'a string'
```

is <false>, because there are two strings but

```
'a string' = 'a string'
```

is <true>, because the two strings are similar.

If you type in the same number twice, POP-11 will not treat the two expressions as denoting two different objects. So 999 will always refer to the same number. Similarly, if you type in the same word twice POP-11 will not treat the two expressions as denoting different objects. When a word is typed in, POP-11 looks in its dictionary to see if it already knows about a word with the characters that have been typed. If it does it assumes that this is the word you meant:

```
"word1" == "word1" =>
** <true>
```

5

Lists

A central thesis of much work in Artificial Intelligence is that computation provides a good — perhaps the best — way to represent cognitive processes such as what we call thinking, seeing, reasoning, speaking and learning. We are obviously not talking about the manipulation of numbers found in much scientific and engineering computation. Intelligence, rather, seems to involve the manipulation of many kinds of symbols which can be used to store information about many kinds of things and their properties and relationships.

Many AI researchers have found that lists are a very general and useful basic structure for storing such information. Lists may contain any type of object, including, for instance, numbers, words, procedures, and other lists. There is no limit to the degree of complexity of the information that they can be used to represent. For instance, the POP-11 database (see Chapter 9) is a list of lists, and operations on the database are simply operations on lists.

These brief remarks do not do justice to the topic, they are intended only as motivation for what is inevitably rather a formal presentation. This chapter introduces several things you need to know about lists, extending the material introduced in Chapter 1. Areas covered are:

(i) The basic operations available for extracting information.
(ii) How lists are represented in memory.
(iii) How to construct them using ::, <> and [...].
(iv) How to test them to see if they satisfy certain conditions.

5.1 BASIC OPERATIONS ON LISTS

The first element of a list is often referred to as its 'head', and is accessed by the built-in POP-11 procedure hd:

```
hd([1 2 3 4]) =>
** 1
```

The first element may be another list:

```
hd([[1 2 3] 4 5]) =>
** [1 2 3]
```

The procedure tl (read as 'tail') is given a list as input and produces as its result a new list, containing all but the first element of the original list:

```
tl([a b c d e]) =>
** [b c d e]
```

Note that the tail of a two element list is a list containing the second element. It is not the second element itself. For example:

```
tl([a b]) =>
** [b]
```

Compare this with:

```
hd(tl([a b])) =>
** b
```

Accessing anything other than the first element requires us to combine together successive applications of hd, or of hd and tl. We illustrate this using the variable building, below:

```
vars building;
[[shed house inn] barn hotel] -> building;
```

To access the word shed, we can do:

```
hd(hd(building)) =>
** shed
```

POP-11 tackles this in several stages, working from the inside out:

(i) ...(...(building))
gets the value of building, which is the list
[[shed house inn] barn hotel]

(ii) ...(hd(...))
does the first (innermost) hd to building. The first element of it is
[shed house inn] . This is now available for

(iii) hd(... (...))
which does the final (outer) hd operation to select its first element, which is the word shed.

An alternative to using hd is to pretend that the list variable, in this case building, is a procedure, and apply it to the number 1 to get the first element. For example:

```
building(1) =>
** [shed house inn]
```

Similarly to get the second and subsequent elements:

```
building(2) =>
** barn

building(3) =>
** hotel

building(4) =>
```

The latter imperative will produce a mishap message because building only contains three elements.

To get the second element of the first element of building do:

```
building(1)(2) =>
** house
```

If you apply hd or tl to an empty list, you will get a mishap message:

```
tl([]) =>

;;; MISHAP - NON-EMPTY LIST NEEDED
;;; INVOLVING:  []
;;; DOING    :  tl compile
```

Notice the lack of symmetry between hd and tl. hd(building) is the same as building(1), but tl(building) is not the same as building(2): it is a list of remaining elements, or [ ] if there are no more.

Moving around lists using hd and tl can be clumsy and laborious, though the consistency and simplicity of these two primitive operations is an attractive feature. We shall see later that we have much more expressive ways of accessing list contents with the procedure matches. Underneath these more powerful modes of list processing there are, however, always the basic operations hd and tl.

dest

One common use of hd and tl is for inspecting each element of a list in turn, using a loop like:

```
until    list == nil
do       hd(list) -> x;        ;;; Get the first element of the list.
         tl(list) -> list;     ;;; Remove this first element from it.
         ...                   ;;; Do whatever you want to X
enduntil;
```

The procedure dest allows you to get the head and tail in one go. It returns two results, one of which is the head and the other the tail, so the above loop could be abbreviated to:

```
until    list == nil
do       dest(list) -> list -> x;
         ...
enduntil;
```

Note the order in which you make use of the results of dest.

null

The procedure null tests whether something is the empty list. It should be used instead of comparing the list with nil if (i) there is any possibility that the target is not in fact a list — null produces a mishap message if given anything other than a list, or (ii) the list may be a 'dynamic' list (see Section 10.6), since such objects will never be equal to nil no matter what you do to them.

last

The procedure last finds the final element of a list:

```
last([cat dog mouse]) =>
** mouse
```

When last is applied to a list of lists, it produces as its result a list, that is, the last list:

```
last([[tom brown] [mary green] [suzy white]]) =>
** [suzy white]
```


rev

The procedure rev, when given a list, produces a new version which has the same elements, but in reverse order:

```
rev([1 2 3 4]) =>
** [4 3 2 1]

hd(rev([cat dog mouse])) =>
** mouse
```

rev does not alter the order of elements in embedded lists:

```
rev([[tom brown] [mary green] [suzy white]]) =>
** [[suzy white] [mary green] [tom brown]]
```

You will find an exercise in Chapter 6 to write a procedure which behaves like rev. At the end of Chapter 7 is an exercise to write a procedure which reverses lists at all levels.

oneof

The procedure oneof chooses an element of a given list at random. Thus using it on different occasions to do apparently the same thing may, or may not, produce different results:

```
oneof([eeny meeny miney moe]) =>
** meeny

oneof([eeny meeny miney moe]) =>
** moe

oneof([eeny meeny miney moe]) =>
** moe
```

Note that oneof is defined in terms of random. As with random, the behaviour of oneof can be made repeatable by initialising ranseed.

delete

The procedure delete produces a copy of a list minus a certain element. delete takes two arguments. The first can be any item, but the second must be a list. It produces one result, a list. For example, to delete the number 3 from a list we can do:

```
delete(3, [1 2 3 4]) =>
** [1 2 4]
```

To delete a word from a list we can do:

```
delete("three", [I saw three ships]) =>
** [I saw ships]
```

The quote marks are necessary, outside list expressions, to ensure that "three" is interpreted as the word "three", and not the value of a variable called three.

delete normally deletes all occurrences of the target item. So it produces an empty list if the second argument contains only occurrences of the first argument, thus:

```
delete(3, [3 3 3]) =>
** []
```

To make delete stop before it has deleted all instances of the target, give it an extra argument specifying how many to delete. For example:

```
delete(3, [3 3 3], 1) =>
** [3 3]

delete(3, [3 3 3], 2) =>
** [3]
```

maplist

The procedure maplist takes a list and a procedure as arguments. It creates a new list by applying the procedure to each element of the given list in turn, and collecting the results together. For example, if we wanted to add 1 to every element in a list of numbers, we might do:

```
define addone(x) -> result;
    x + 1 -> result;
enddefine;

maplist([2 4 6 8 10], addone) =>
** [3 5 7 9 11]
```

maplist is an example of a procedure with a procedural argument. It is used to do whatever the procedural argument says should be done to each member of the list, and to make a new list out of the results. We will see later examples of things which can be done easily using procedures with procedural arguments, which would otherwise be almost impossible.

applist

applist takes a list and a procedure as argument. It applies the procedure to every element in the list. Unlike maplist, it does not return the results in a list, as shown below:

```
applist([2 4 6 8 10], addone) =>
** 3 5 7 9 11
```

appdata

The procedure appdata works in the same way as applist. The only difference is that the first input argument can be any kind of data structure — not just a list. For example, it might be a vector:

```
appdata({2 4 6 8 10}, addone) =>
** 3 5 7 9 11
```

If you use appdata on a list, the effect is slightly surprising:

```
appdata([1 2 3 4], spr);
```

returns:

```
1 [2 3 4]
```

This is because lists, as we will see in the next section, are actually represented as chains of two element cells. The head of the list is kept in the first element of the first cell, and a pointer to the tail is kept in the second. appdata looks at the object it has been given, sees that it is a two element cell, and applies its procedural argument to the two elements of this cell, that is, the head and tail of the list.

datalist

The procedure datalist takes a data structure as argument, and makes a list out of its components. It makes use of another built-in procedure, explode. explode takes a data structure as argument, and puts all its components on the stack. datalist and explode are not defined for every possible data type, but they do work for strings, words, lists, vectors, and user-defined data types. They could be defined something like:

```
define explode(x);
    if      islist(x)
    then    applist(x, identfn);
    else    appdata(x, identfn);
    endif;
enddefine;

define datalist(x);
    [% explode(x) %]
enddefine;
```

The test in explode to see if the argument is a list is to prevent it using appdata, since, as we have seen, the effect of appdata on a list is not what you would normally want. identfn is a procedure which takes a single argument and returns it unchanged — it is useful for things like explode. The use of the % symbol in lists is explained in Section 5.3.2.

5.2 THE STRUCTURE OF LISTS IN MEMORY

This section is included in order to give you some understanding of how lists are represented within the computer's memory. A simple introduction is important if you wish to appreciate how the representation permits such a flexible data structure, and how basic operations on lists are made possible.

You would usually expect to write your programs using the high level facilities for manipulating lists, which conceal the details of how they are represented in the machine from you. It is nevertheless worth trying to understand how lists are really represented, since it can make it easier to understand what has gone wrong with your program when you get mishap messages; and it can help you to make fuller use of the flexibility that using lists provides.

The computer's memory consists of a collection of 'boxes'. (These are sometimes called 'words'. We will talk about 'boxes' to avoid confusion with the POP-11 'words' which we have already discussed, which are entirely different things.) These are locations where information can be stored. A 'pair' is an object (or 'record') which contains two arbitrary POP-11 data items called the 'front' and the 'back'. Pairs may be used in their own right for any purpose, but their most frequent use is to represent lists of items. In POP-11, a list is represented as a chain of pairs. The front and back of each pair occupy consecutive boxes in memory, whereas the individual pairs may be scattered all over memory. The front of each pair in the chain is used to hold the next element of the list. The back holds the continuation of the chain, which may be either another pair, or the special item nil, indicating the end of the list. The two parts of the pair are then known as the 'head' and the 'tail' respectively. Thus, whereas the head of a list can be any item, the tail must always be another list (nil is considered to be a list). nil in POP-11 can be written as [ ], which is how an empty list is printed out.

We use box diagrams to represent the structure of lists in memory. One box represents one location in memory. We can represent the result of executing the imperative

```
vars x;
[a b] -> x;
```

as follows:

vars x tells the computer to associate a portion of memory with the word x, which is stored in the dictionary. Next the expression [a b] causes POP-11 to construct two linked pairs, thus:

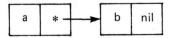

a denotes a pointer to the word a, b to the word b, and nil to the special object signifying the end of the list. When the chain has been built, POP-11 leaves the address of the first link on the stack. Next the assignment —> x causes the address to be removed from the stack and copied into the memory location associated with the word x. This is illustrated below:

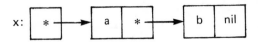

 indicates that the number (or 'address') of the first pair of boxes is stored in the box associated with the word x.

The following actions first access the value of the variable x, and then access the contents of the pairs:

```
vars y;
x -> y;       ;;; copy address of list to Y
hd(y) =>      ;;; print out front of first pair
** A
tl(y) -> y; ;;; copy back of first pair to Y
hd(y) =>      ;;; print front of second pair
** B
tl(y) -> y; ;;; copy back of second pair to Y
hd(y) =>
;;; MISHAP - NON-EMPTY LIST NEEDED
;;; INVOLVING:  []
;;; DOING     : hd compile
y =>
** []
```

When the address assigned to x is accessed, the first pair of boxes is found. The front of the pair contains the address of a series of boxes representing the word a, the back contains the address of a second pair of boxes. The front of the second pair contains the address of the boxes representing the word b. The back contains the address of the special object nil.

In the following example, a list containing two lists and a word is represented. Note that the address of nil is stored three times:

`[[THE MAN] KICKED [A DOG]] -> x;`

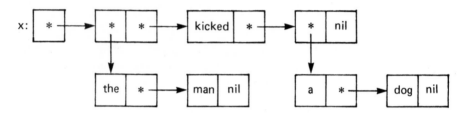

Exercise
1. Draw the box diagrams corresponding to:
    (i) [[[a]]]
    (ii) [a [b [c [d]]]]
    Hint: there should be an occurrence of nil for each right bracket.

5.3   CONSTRUCTING LISTS

The simplest way to construct a list is to use square brackets, but there are several others.

5.3.1   The use of [...]
These 'list constant brackets', [. . .], may contain text items, like words, numbers, strings, lists, or anything else. For example

`[a b c d]`

is a list of four words, and

`[string 'a short string' 66]`

is a list with a word, a string and a number. [ ] is the empty list, and is the value of the system identifier nil.

List brackets may also be used to construct lists which contain lists. For example [[1 2] [3] 4] is a three element list, containing a number and two lists containing numbers.

5.3.2   The use of % in list expressions
The percent symbol, %, can be used to create lists whose contents depend on the values of variables or the results of executing imperatives. For example

`[% 3, cat, hd(l) %] -> x;`

is a list containing the number 3, the value of the variable cat and the first element of l, which must be a list, whereas

```
[3, cat, hd(l)]
```

contains the number 3, the comma, the word "cat", another comma, the word "hd", the word "(", and so on.

```
[% [% a %], [% b, c%], [% d %] %]
```

is a list of three lists, whose contents depend on the values of a, b, c and d.

In POP-11, the percent symbol may appear anywhere in a list. This makes it easy to mix words and text to be taken literally, with bits of program to be executed. For example:

```
[the sum of 666 and 777 is % 666 + 777 % exactly] =>
** [the sum of 666 and 777 is 1443 exactly]
```

In this example we have embedded an expression to be evaluated in among the various constant items which are to be left as they are. We can include several pairs of % signs, as in:

```
[two plus three is % 2+3 % whereas three plus two is % 2+3 %] =>
** [two plus three is 5 whereas three plus two is 5]
```

Every opening % sign must be matched by a closing one.

5.3.3 The use of ^ (the 'up-arrow' or 'hat' symbol)

The symbols ^ and ^^ can be used to do much the same thing as %. ^(. . .) can be used in place of %. . .%. For example:

```
[the sum of 666 and 777 is ^(666 + 777) exactly] =>
** [the sum of 666 and 777 is 1443 exactly]
```

The parentheses after ^ can be omitted if they contain only one item:

```
[^X + ^Y is ^(X + Y)]
```

is the same as

```
[% X, "+", Y, "is", X + Y %]
```

or

```
[% X % + % Y % is % X + Y %]
```

When followed by a variable, ^ means 'use the value of this variable'. When followed by a parenthesised expression it means, 'use the value of the parenthesised expression'.

5.3.4 The use of ^^ ('double up-arrow' symbol)

This is used to merge the contents of a list into an enclosing list. Thus:

```
vars list;
[ b c d ] -> list;

[a ^list e ] =>
** [a [b c d] e]
```

Compare this with:

```
[a ^^list e ] =>
** [a b c d e]
```

The single ^ followed by a variable inserts a single element into a list. The element will be the value of the variable, even if it is a list. By contrast, ^^ followed by a variable whose value is a list inserts the elements of the list separately. The prefix ^^ can be thought of as 'remove the list brackets'. If the value is not a list, an error will result. For example:

```
vars x;
99 -> x;

[a b c ^^x] =>

;;; MISHAP - LIST NEEDED
;;; INVOLVING:   99
;;; DOING     :  compile
```

The procedure list_nums_to, below, illustrates the use of ^ and ^^. It makes a list of integers from 1 up to a given number, n, in descending order:

```
define list_nums_to(n) -> list;
    vars num;
    [] -> list;   ;;; start with empty list
    for num from 1 to n do
        [^num ^^list] -> list;
    endfor;
enddefine;
```

To call list_nums_to with the argument 5, do:

```
list_nums_to(5) =>
** [5 4 3 2 1]
```

Exercise
2.   Alter the above example to produce a list in ascending order.

Just as ^ can be followed by a parenthesised expression, so can ^^, provided that the expression evaluates to a list. For example:

```
[a b c d] -> x;

[the tail of x contains the elements: ^^(tl(x))] ==>
** [the tail of x contains the elements : b c d]
```

Exercise

3.   Suppose the value of x is a one element list [cat]. Then what is the list:

[sam is a ^(hd(x))]

How could an equivalent list be constructed using ^^ instead of ^?

5.3.5 The operation :: (cons)

The procedure ::, called 'cons', makes a new list by joining an element onto an existing list. It is an infix operator whose second argument must be a list. For example:

```
vars x, y;
[4 5 6] -> x;
3 -> y;

y :: x  =>
** [3 4 5 6]

"CAT" :: [] =>
** [CAT]

"CAT" :: "DOG" =>

;;; MISHAP - LIST NEEDED
;;; INVOLVING:  DOG
;;; DOING    :  :: compile nextitem compile
```

The result of the operation y :: x —> z can be expressed, using boxes to represent memory locations, as follows:

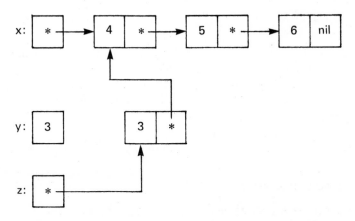

The diagram shows that y has the value 3 which is then copied into the front of a new pair, the back of which holds the address of the first pair of x. z holds the address of the new pair, whose back points to the same pair as the variable x. x and y still have their original values. Note that $y::x$ is equivalent to [^y ^^x]. The way that the structures denoted by the two expressions are represented in memory is identical. The POP-11 compiler recognises that the double up-arrow at the end of the list means that the list value can be appended to the new list and thus saves it having to be copied. It is a matter of personal preference which syntax is used.

5.3.6 The procedure conspair

The procedure conspair can be thought of as equivalent to ::. That is,

```
conspair(x, l)
```

is the same as:

```
x :: l
```

The only difference is that the second argument of conspair need not be a list. For example:

```
conspair(3, 4) -> l;
l =>
** [3|4]
```

3 :: 4 would have produced a LIST NEEDED mishap message.

Note the presence of the vertical bar when l is printed out. This indicates that the number 4 is not the second element of the list, as in [3 4]. Rather, this is not a list at all, since a non-empty list must have as its tail, or back, another list, possibly the empty list. l now has 4 as its back, and 4 is not a list. Attempting to treat l as a list, by asking for its tl, for example, produces a mishap because tl insists on a proper list. A pair whose second element is not a pair is not acceptable to tl. The procedure back has no such qualms:

```
back(l) =>
** 4
```

You can use conspair if you are working with two element data structures, which can be appropriately represented as pairs. Rarely use it for list manipulation since it fails to detect situations where you think you are adding something to the front of a list, but in fact the item you are adding to is not a list. For example:

```
vars l; [1 2 3 4] -> l; ;;; declare L, assign a list to it

3 :: l1 =>                ;;; try to add 3 to it, but misspelt L
;;; DECLARING VARIABLE l1

;;; MISHAP - LIST NEEDED    ;;; :: reports an error
;;; INVOLVING: <undef l1>
;;; DOING    : :: compile nextitem compile

conspair(3, l1) =>        ;;; whereas CONSPAIR is quite happy with L1
** [3|<undef l1>]
```

Experts sometimes use conspair instead of :: for efficiency, along with front and back instead of hd and tl, and destpair instead of dest. These all run a bit faster, but do less checking. (fast_front and fast_back do even less checking. Experts may use them in fully debugged programs, at their own risk!)

POP-11 includes mechanisms for creating and using 'dynamic lists', whose elements are created as needed by a generator procedure. This is sometimes referred to as lazy evaluation. Only hd and tl can be used to access the first element and remainder of a dynamic list. (See Section 10.6).

5.3.7 The operation <> (concatenate)

This procedure, called the 'concatenator', produces a new list by concatenating two lists. Below are the lists lista and listb:

```
vars lista, listb;
[cat dog] -> lista;
[pig mouse] -> listb;
```

To make a new list, listc, containing the elements of lista and the elements of listb we do:

```
lista <> listb -> listc;

listc =>
** [cat dog pig mouse]
```

How the effects of this operation appear in memory is shown below:

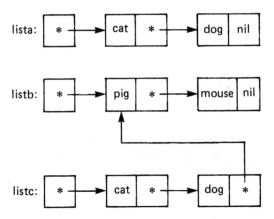

To make listc, lista is copied, but instead of the back of the last pair being nil, there is a pointer to the front of the first pair of listb. Since the first list, lista, is copied, the original value of the variable lista is unchanged. Hence:

```
lista =>
** [cat dog]

listb =>
** [pig mouse]
```

Thus

```
[^x] <> l -> l;
```

is the same in effect as

```
x :: l -> l;
```
or

```
[^x ^^l] -> l;
```

except that [^x] <> l first creates the list [^x] and then <> copies it. It then discards the original. This means that where the original list is not needed for later use, it is less efficient to use <>. In [^^l ^x] the list l is also copied. Notice that

```
x <> y
```

is equivalent to:

```
[^^x ^^y]
```

The operator <> is a very general procedure which can also be used to join two words, two vectors, two strings and even two procedures. Examples follow:

Words:
```
"cat" <> "catcher" = "catcatcher" =>
** <true>
```

Vectors:
```
{one two} <> {three four} =>
** {one two three four}
```

Strings:
```
'a string' <> ' and another' =>
** a string and another
```

Procedures:
It is sometimes useful to define a procedure in terms of two others which it applies in succession. For example, a procedure to compute the square root of a number and then print it out could be defined thus:

```
define prsqrt(x);
    pr(sqrt(x));
enddefine;
```

A slightly more efficient and more compact version could be created by:

```
vars procedure prsqrt;
sqrt <> pr -> prsqrt;
```

After this, prsqrt can be used as if it had been defined as a procedure identifier:

```
prsqrt(10);
3.16228
```

Exercises

4. Write down some examples of expressions denoting:

    (i) a list of numbers

    (ii) a list of words

    (iii) a list of numbers and words

    (iv) a list of lists of words

    (v) a list of lists of numbers.

5. What is denoted by each of the following:

```
i.     hd([once upon a time])
ii.    last([mary had a little lamb])
iii.   hd([[mary had] [a little lamb]])
iv.    rev([mary had a little lamb])
v.     last(hd([[mary had] [a little lamb]]))
vi.    delete("cat", [mouse pig cat dog])
vii.   last(hd([[tom brown] [mary green] [suzy white]]))
viii.  last(last([[tom brown] [mary green] [suzy white]]))
ix.    hd(hd([[tom brown] [mary green] [suzy white]]))
x.     hd(tl([[tom brown] [mary green] [suzy white]]))
xi.    tl(hd([[tom brown] [mary green] [suzy white]]))
xii.   tl(tl([[tom brown] [mary green] [suzy white]]))
```

6. What does oneof do?

7. What does delete do?

8. What do the following denote:

```
delete(3, rev([1 2 3 4 5]))

rev(delete("little", [mary had a little lamb]))
```

9. Using delete and oneof define a procedure to deal cards from a pack. The procedure will take two arguments, a list and a number. The list will represent the cards in the pack, and the number will specify how many cards are to be dealt. Each time a card is dealt it must be deleted from the pack so that it cannot be redealt. The card value must also be printed out when it is dealt.

10. If we assign [a b] to x, thus:

```
[a b] -> x;
```

then the list [^^x c] is [a b c], and the list [^x c] is [[a b] c].

What values would have to be assigned to x, y etc. so that the following were <true> (some are impossible — which ones?):

```
[^^x ^^x] = [a b a b]      ;;; answer is [A B] -> X;
[^x ^^y] = [[a b] b c]     ;;; answer is [A B] -> X; [B C] -> Y;
```

```
i.     [^^x mother ^^y] = [i love my mother]
ii.    [the height of steve is ^^x] = [the height of steve is 6 ft]
iii.   [every ^^x is a ^^y] = [every fire man is a civil servant]
iv.    [every ^x is a ^y] = [every fire man is a civil servant]
v.     [^^x i ^^y you] = [sometimes i hate people like you]
vi.    [[^x ^^y] ^^z] = [[a b c d]]
vii.   [^x [^^y] ^z] = [[a b] [c d] [e f]]
```

viii. [i saw ^^n ships] = [i saw 3 ships]
ix.   [i saw ^n ships] = [i saw 3 ships]
x.   [i ^x you] = [i hate computers]
xi.   [^x ^y ^z] = [i hate computers]

If you have access to a computer, use it to check your answers. For example, if you think the answer to the second one is

[6 feet] -> x;

then try printing the list:

[the height of steve is ^^x] =>

Later you will see that the procedure matches can be used to find the answers.

Procedures and other control facilities

This chapter describes in more detail the syntax of POP-11 procedure definitions, and of compound expressions and imperatives such as loops, conditionals and switch statements. In order to make the reader more familiar with the list data structure, procedures manipulating lists are used in the examples.

6.1 DEFINING PROCEDURES

We have already seen some examples of procedure definitions, for example doublesum and silly. Here is a specification of the format for a procedure definition:

```
define <name of procedure>
       (<input locals in parentheses, separated by commas>)
       -> <output local> (if required)
       ;
       <action>s to be performed (forming the "body"). These may
       include conditionals, loops, nested procedures, and so on.
enddefine;
```

Note that if there are no input locals, the parentheses in the heading will be empty. These parentheses are always optional, and they are often omitted in cases where they would have been empty.

This format is 'bracketed' by two keywords, define and enddefine. This is a common pattern in POP-11. We have seen several other examples already, for example if and endif, and for and endfor. (These cases also have 'separating'

keywords, so that the complete pattern for for loops is for . . . do . . . endfor.)
Expressions immediately preceding a separating keyword like do or then must
not end with a semicolon. The semicolon before a closing keyword, however,
is optional. In the remainder of the book we will include it, or omit it, as seems
most appropriate.

Below is a procedure, addtwo, which takes two numbers as input, and produces a new number by adding them:

```
define addtwo(num1, num2);
    num1 + num2;
enddefine;
```

This definition produces a result, even though it does not use an output local.
This is because the procedure calls +, which leaves its result on the stack. Since
the result of + is not removed from the stack, it is left as the result of addtwo
also.

We can indicate more clearly that a procedure is to produce a result by using
an output local variable in the procedure heading, as we have done previously.
For example:

```
define addtwo2(num1, num2) -> result;
    num1 + num2 -> result;
enddefine;
```

Though clearer, this is marginally less efficient, since it has an extra local variable,
and does an extra assignment and stack operation. The loss of efficiency is very
slight, and should only be allowed to outweigh the gain in clarity for particularly
important procedures.

Procedures with more than one output local

If a procedure is to return one or more results, it can be given output locals. We
have already seen examples of procedures with one output local variable, for
example addtwo2 and perim. Sometimes it is convenient to have a procedure
produce more than one result. For example, the procedure stats, below, takes a
list of numbers and produces both the sum of all the numbers, and their average.
The two results are left on the stack when the procedure exits:

```
define stats(numlist) -> sum -> average;
    vars item;
    0 -> sum;
    for item in numlist do
        item + sum -> sum;
    endfor;
    sum/length(numlist) -> average
enddefine;

vars s a;
stats([1 3 5 9]) -> s -> a;  ;;; note that the order is the same
                             ;;; as in the procedure definition
```

```
s =>
** 18
a =>
** 4.5
```

Note that output locals are like ordinary local variables in that the values assigned to them during execution of the procedure are not available after the procedure has finished, as may be seen if you try to access the values of sum and average below:

```
sum =>
** <undef sum>
average =>
** <undef average>
```

Assignments to output locals can happen anywhere in the procedure. When the procedure finishes, the values of the output locals at that time are left on the stack. In the example above, the values are taken off the stack after the procedure stats finishes, and POP-11 assigns them to s and to a. Note that the order in which they are put on the stack is the reverse of the order in which they occur in the procedure heading. The order of the assignments to take them off the stack is the same as the order in the procedure heading. Thus the procedure heading gives the format for a typical call of the procedure in which the results are assigned. When you are trying to work out the order in which to use the results of a multiple result procedure, it is easier to copy the order in which they appear in the procedure heading than to try to work it out from first principles by reasoning about the stack.

You have now seen how you would usually define procedures. POP-11 provides two variations on the standard format which are very useful in specialised circumstances. One variation allows you to define anonymous procedures. The other allows you to treat a procedure as a local variable.

The procedure syntax

The word procedure can be used to introduce an anonymous procedure. The format is:

```
procedure(<input locals>) -> <output locals>;
    <body>
endprocedure;
```

The <output locals> are optional. The procedure is left on the stack. It may be applied immediately. For example:

```
procedure(x); x + 1 => endprocedure (7);
** 8
```

You can assign the procedure to a variable using this syntax by doing:

```
vars addone; procedure(x); x + 1 endprocedure -> addone;
addone(7) =>
** 8
```

This would be a fairly unusual way to use an anonymous procedure, since it has immediately been given a name. A more common use is as argument to maplist, applist, or appdata, where there is something which you want to embody as a procedure so that you can apply it to every member of some data structure. If you are not going to need the procedure anywhere else, there is little point in giving it a name, for example:

```
maplist([4 6 5 3], procedure(x); x - 1 endprocedure) =>
** [3 5 4 2]
```

They are also used when constructing a table of procedures which will be accessed by position rather than by name. Programs which themselves write other programs may also create anonymous procedures.

Locally defining procedures

Just as you can declare variables to be local to procedures, so you can define procedures to be local to procedures. A procedure name in POP-11 is a variable. The value of the name is the procedure. Locally defined procedures can only be accessed from the procedure within which they are defined. If you can be sure that you know the only place where some procedure is ever going to be called, defining it locally can lead to elegant programs. It also helps you avoid potential name clashes with other procedures. For example, the procedure big_num is locally defined inside the procedure big_num_row, below. big_num_row takes a list of numbers as input, and prints them in a row if they are all bigger than 100, otherwise it mishaps:

```
define big_num_row (list);
    define big_num(num);
        if      num < 100
        then    mishap('Number not greater than 100', [^num ^list])
        else    spr(num);
        endif;
    enddefine;
    applist(list, big_num)
enddefine;
```

We can now try it out:

```
big_num_row([198 87687 23425 1235]);
198 87687 23425 1235
```

big_num_row would have run perfectly successfully even if there had been a previous definition of big_num, since big_num_row makes use of its own local version. Since this version is local, running big_num_row would have made no difference to the previously defined version.

Locally redefining procedures

Procedures may also be locally redefined. This allows you to modify existing procedures so that they behave in a unique way when called from the outer procedure. Consider the following procedure:

```
define check_list(input_list) -> output_list;
    vars x;
    [% for x in input_list
        do   check_it(x)
        endfor %] -> output_list;
enddefine;
```

The effect of this procedure depends on what check_it does. We can define various procedures which locally redefine check_it and then call check_list:

```
define get_biggest(input_list) -> output_list;
    define check_it(x);
        max(x(1), x(2));
    enddefine;
    check_list(input_list) -> output_list;
enddefine;

define get_smallest(input_list) -> output_list;
    define check_it(x);
        min(x(1), x(2));
    enddefine;
    check_list(input_list) -> output_list;
enddefine;
```

Each of these provides its own local definition of check_it (using the system procedures max and min, which each take two numbers and return the larger and smaller respectively), which is the version that check_list will use. So:

```
vars list ;
[[1 3] [6 100] [2 -9] [77 66]] -> list;
get_biggest(list) =>
** [3 100 2 77]
get_smallest(list) =>
** [1 6 -9 66]
```

Locally redefining procedures is particularly useful when you are defining procedures to change the standard input and output facilities. There is an example in Section 12.4.1.

Premature exit from procedures

All procedure definitions contain a 'body', that is, some instructions between the define and the enddefine. In the examples used so far in this chapter, all the instructions in the body are executed and then the procedure terminates. We saw in Section 1.2 that it is possible for a procedure to terminate early if the expression return() is present. For example:

```
define very_silly();
    vars x;
    2 -> x;
    return();
    x =>
enddefine;

very_silly() =>
**
```

very_silly would have printed out the value of x, namely 2, but the presence of return prevented it ever getting that far, so in fact it prints nothing. This illustrates an important point about return − it is seldom sensible to use it anywhere other than in a condition expression (see below). The pattern

```
if <test> then <action> return(); endif;
```

is so common that exit is provided as an abbreviation for return( ); endif; as in:

```
if <test> then <action> exit
```

return may take a number of arguments. These become the results of the procedure which is being exited from. If the procedure has output locals, these are treated as though the procedure had exited normally, that is, they are returned as results. If you use return (or exit) with arguments within a procedure that also has output locals, you will get very confused about the order in which all the results are returned.

We will return to the topic of alternative ways of exiting from a procedure in Section 14.2.

6.2 COMPOUND EXPRESSIONS AND IMPERATIVES

Having established the syntax of POP-11 procedures, we now introduce the different structures available for determining how and when instructions in the body of procedures are carried out. In this chapter we concentrate on conditionals and the commonly used iterative syntactic forms. Chapter 7 introduces recursion.

6.2.1 Conditionals

Conditionals have several forms, but the <condition> part is always an expression which must evaluate to <true> or <false>. If it is <true> the <action> is carried out. If it is <false> the <action> is not carried out. Different forms of conditionals are illustrated below:

i.   `if <condition> then <action> endif`

ii.   `if <condition> then <action1> else <action2> endif`

(ii) says, if the <condition> is <true>, then execute <action1>, otherwise execute <action2>.

iii.
```
if <condition1> then <action1>
    elseif <condition2> then <action2>
    elseif <condition3> then <action3>
    elseunless <condition4> then <action4>
    ...
    ...
    else <default action>
endif;
```

This 'multi-branch' conditional says, if <condition1> is <true>, execute <action1>. Otherwise, try <condition2>, <condition3>, and so on, until either an elseif <condition> is found which is <true>, or an elseunless <condition> is found which is <false>. If either is found, execute the corresponding <action>. If none of the conditions return <true>, do the action following else, that is, the <default action>.

Note that in an imperative the else <default action> bit may be left out. You must, however, have it in an expression intended to denote something, for then it should denote something under all conditions. You can include as many elseif clauses as you like.

    iv.   `unless <condition> then <action> endunless`

is equivalent to:

    `if not(<condition>) then <action> endif`

unless can also have elseunless, elseif and else clauses. Combining if with elseunless, or unless with elseif can get confusing.

The words not, and and or are available for use in formulating complex conditions. For example:

    `if <condition1> or (<condition2> and not(<condition3>))`

A conditional imperative may leave something on the stack. It can then play the role of an expression denoting an object. For example, if x and y have numbers as values, the larger can be assigned to the variable bigger by the following:

    `if x < y then y else x endif -> bigger;`

In some cases this can lead to clearer programs, in other cases it leads to ones which are hard to read. It is up to you to choose which is more sensible in a given context. You can also use conditional expressions as the destinations of assignments, as in:

    `n -> if n < 10 then x else y endif;`

The effect of this would be to make n the value of x if n was less than 10, and otherwise to make it the value of y. The situations in which writing things like this makes your program easier to read and understand are less common, though it can occasionally be useful.

Examples
To test whether the value of x is bigger than the value of y, and then print out the bigger value, do:

    `if  x > y  then  x =>  else  y =>  endif;`

The same effect could have been achieved by:

    `if x > y then x else y endif =>`

A more discriminatory conditional could have been expressed as:

```
if        x > y
then      x =>
elseif    y > x
then      y =>
else      "same" =>
endif;
```

or

```
if x > y then x elseif y > x then y else "same" endif =>
```

The following illustrates a case where using a conditional as the target of an assignment might be reasonable:

```
x -> if  x > list(1) then list(1) else list(2) endif;
```

This says make x the head of the list if it is greater than the current head, otherwise make it the second element. If you find this confusing, you should stick to the more normal form:

```
if      x > list(1)
then    x -> list(1)
else    x -> list(2)
endif;
```

When an if statement is used simply to return <true> or <false>, the <condition> part alone could form the expression. So

```
if    2 < x and x < 6
then  true
else  false
endif =>
```

is equivalent to:

```
2 < x and x < 6  =>
```

6.2.2 Loops: instructions to do something repeatedly

To make POP-11 do some instructions several times, we usually use a looping construct. These constructs are also known as 'iterative'. Several forms of iteration are introduced below:

until <condition> do <action> enduntil

This means, check if the <condition> is <true>. If it is not <true> then do the <action>. Then test again to see if the <condition> is <true>, and so on. The <condition> is tested again each time after the <action> is done. For example, to print out all the numbers from 3 to 99, you can do:

```
vars num;
3 -> num;
```

```
until num > 99 do
    num =>
    num + 1 -> num;
enduntil;
```

The <action> part of a loop may be an arbitrarily complex POP-11 imperative, or sequence of imperatives, just as for conditionals. So, to print out the words 'the', 'cat', 'sat', 'on', 'the', and 'mat', we could put them in a list, and print out each element. We achieve this by using the system procedure tl. Each time around the loop the first element of the list is printed, and then chopped off, until the list is empty. The procedure traverse, below, does this:

```
define traverse(list);
    vars list;
    until list = []
    do  spr(hd(list));           ;;; print first element
        tl(list) -> list;        ;;; prepare for next
    enduntil;
enddefine;
```

Doing

```
traverse([the cat sat on the mat]);
```

prints the following:

```
the cat sat on the mat
```

Note that the loop will not be terminated immediately if the <condition> becomes <true> in the middle of executing the <action>. Also, the <condition> is always tested at least once before anything else is done.

while <condition> do <action> endwhile
This means, test the <condition>. If it is <true>, then do the <action>. Then test the <condition> again, and so on. This is similar to until, except that while does the <action> as long as the <condition> is <true>, whereas until does the <action> as long as the <condition> is <false>. In both cases the <condition> is tested first. For example, to find the first integer whose square is greater than 1000, you could do:

```
vars num;
1 -> num;
while num * num < 1000 do
    num + 1 -> num
endwhile;
```

The value of num and its square can now be printed out:

```
num =>
** 32

num * num =>
** 1024
```

repeat <expression> times <action> endrepeat
After the word repeat you can have any expression that denotes a number. The <action> is repeated the specified number of times. For example, to print out 10 blank lines, you can do:

```
repeat 10 times pr(newline) endrepeat;
```

The <expression> is evaluated only once. For example, if it is a variable whose value changes in the course of the <action>, the <action> is repeated as many times as the variable's initial value:

```
vars n; 3 -> n;
repeat n times n => n + 1 -> n endrepeat;
** 3
** 4
** 5
```

If you leave out the numeric expression, the iteration will continue for ever. The format is:

```
repeat <action> endrepeat
```

For example:

```
repeat
    [you are wonderful] =>
endrepeat;
```

If you type the above to POP-11, it will keep printing out

```
** [you are wonderful]
```

until you interrupt it, for example by typing <ctrl>&C. The format

```
repeat forever [you are wonderful] => endrepeat;
```

is equivalent, but makes it clearer that the loop has no termination condition.

for . . . endfor loops
We have seen examples of the use of the for . . . endfor construction to iterate over lists, for example in find_and_show_all, in Section 1.2. Strictly, for is redundant, since we can always use while or until loops instead. However, for loops are usually more compact, and make it easier for a reader to see what the program is supposed to do. There are several different formats, explained below.

for <x> in <list> do <action> endfor
We often want to refer to each element of a list in turn, doing something with it, such as adding to a running total. To avoid constantly having to use an expression of the form hd(. . .), we 'package up' the instructions using this version of the for loop. For example, to add all the numbers in a list, we could do:

```
define addall(list) -> total;
    vars x;
    0 -> total;
    for x in list do
        x + total -> total
    endfor
enddefine;

addall([3 5 7 9]) =>
** 24
```

Here we do not have to include an explicit assignment of the tail of <list> to <list>, such as

```
tl(list) -> list;
```

since the equivalent of this is implied in the for construct. Note that the variable list is not changed in the loop. A new 'hidden' variable is introduced to point at successive links in the list.

for <x> on <list> do <action> endfor

Here, the first time the <action> is done, x refers to the whole <list>. The second time it refers to the tl of <list>, the next time to the tl of the tl of <list>, and so on. For example:

```
for x on [a b c] do x => endfor;
** [a b c]
** [b c]
** [c]
```

Note that we might have expected x to be printed out one more time, when its value is [ ] . The for loop does not enumerate the case when <list> has been completely exhausted.

Like for <x> in ... do ... endfor, an expression like

```
for <x> on <list> do ... endfor
```

would not change the value of <list> (although it would change the value of x).

for <x> from <expression> by <expression> to <expression> do <action> endfor

The <expression>s in the above must all have numbers as their values. This format enables us to specify loops over ranges of numbers.

The following prints out numbers from 2 to 20 going up in steps of 7:

```
for x from 2 by 7 to 20 do x => endfor;
** 2
** 9
** 16
```

or going down:

```
for x from 50 by -12.5 to -20 do x => endfor;
** 50
** 37.5
** 25.0
** 12.5
** 0.0
** -12.5
```

The from <expression> and by <expression> portions may be omitted. The starting value defaults to 1, as does the increment:

```
vars x;
for x to 6 do pr(x); pr(space) endfor;
1 2 3 4 5 6
```

for <initiate> step <step> till <condition> do <action> endfor
This form of the for loop is equivalent to:

```
<initiate>;
until <condition> do <action>; <step> enduntil;
```

In other words, do the initialisation, then, until the <condition> evaluates to <true>, repeatedly do the <action> followed by the <step>. For example, to print out all the numbers from lo to hi, separated by spaces, you can do:

```
for  lo -> x  step  x+1 -> x till  x > hi  do  spr(x); endfor;
```

Note that the <step> is not done until after the <action>.

Suppose wordnum is a procedure which takes two arguments, namely a word and a number. If you are given a list of words and a list of numbers, and wish to apply wordnum to the first element of each, then the second element of each, and so on, until either there are no more words, or no more numbers, you could do something like:

```
vars w, n;
for words -> w; numbers -> n;
step  tl(w) -> w; tl(n) -> n;
till  w = [] or n = []
do    wordnum(hd(w), hd(n));
endfor;
```

Using for in [%. . .%]
We can use a for loop to define the procedure delete, which takes two inputs, a list, and an item to be removed from the list, and returns the list minus all occurrences of the item. We will use a variable, say x, to denote successive elements in a list. If the element is not the same as the item to be deleted, we will leave the element on the stack. We can use unless to mean if not, as explained above. If all this is done inside the 'decorated list brackets', [%. . .%], then the items left on the stack are made into a list:

```
define delete(item,list) -> result;
    vars x;
    [% for x in list do
        unless x = item then x /* left on stack */  endunless;
    endfor
    %] -> result
enddefine;

delete([a b], [[1 2] [3 4] [a b] [c d]]) =>
** [[1 2] [3 4] [c d]]
```

6.3 PREMATURE EXIT FROM LOOPS

There are a number of formats for specifying, half-way through the action part of a loop, that we want to quit the loop immediately. These are rather similar to the use of return for exiting immediately from a procedure.

quitloop

To jump out of the current loop, the construct quitloop is provided. For example, the procedure lookfor, below, takes a list and an item as input arguments. The item is searched for in the list using a for loop. If the item is found, control jumps from the loop, and a list, indicating that the item has been found, is printed out. If the item is not found, a list indicating this is printed out:

```
define lookfor(list, item);
    vars x, list, item, found;
    false -> found;      ;;; Assume you won't find it
    for x in list        ;;; Inspect each item in turn
    do  if  x = item then
            true -> found;  ;;; Note that you did find it
            quitloop;    ;;; Terminate the FOR loop immediately
        endif;
    endfor;
    if found then        ;;; Was it found ?
        pr([item ^item has been found]);
    else
        pr([item ^item has not been found]);
    endif
enddefine;
```

Calling lookfor with

```
lookfor([1 2 3],4);
```

returns:

```
[item 4 has not been found]

lookfor([1 2 3],2);
```

returns:

```
[item 2 has been found]
```

To quit from more than one loop, provide a number in parentheses after quitloop. For example, if you type

```
for list in embeddedlist
do  for x in list
     do  if      x == target
         then    [Found it] =>
                 quitloop(2)
         endif;
     endfor;
endfor;
[It was in %list%] =>
```

then when an instance of target is found, control passes out of both loops, and execution continues after the end of the outer loop; so the next instruction executed is the one which prints out where the item was found.

quitif
As with return, the most common use of quitloop is inside a conditional imperative. quitif provides a convenient way of using quitloop in such contexts. Control passes from the loop enclosing the instruction

```
quitif(<expression>)
```

if <expression> is <true>. The above is equivalent to:

```
if <expression> then quitloop endif
```

If quitif is followed by an integer, n, control leaves the nth enclosing loop, just as with quitloop. The resulting format looks like:

```
quitif(<expression>) (n)
```

quitunless
quitunless works in the same way as quitif:

```
quitunless(<expression>)(n)
```

is equivalent to

```
unless <expression> then quitloop(n) endunless
```

where n is an optional argument.

nextloop
When nextloop is executed in a looping construct, control jumps to just before the syntax word closing the loop, for example endwhile for a while loop, and endfor for a for loop. This causes the enclosing loop to be restarted. Consider the procedure, no_increase, below:

```
define no_increase();
    vars x;
    1 -> x;
    while x =< 10 do
        x =>
        nextloop;    ;;; Jump to just before ENDWHILE
        x + 1 -> x; ;;; this instruction is never done
    endwhile
enddefine;
```

If we call no_increase it will go on for ever, simply typing out ** 1 over and over again, until it is interrupted from the outside, for instance by your typing <ctrl>&C.

If nextloop is followed by an integer, n, the nth enclosing loop is restarted.

Just as with return and quitloop, nextloop is usually used inside a conditional imperative. nextif and nextunless are provided for packaging up conditional expressions involving nextloop. They are analogous to quitif and quitunless.

6.4 ARBITRARY TRANSFER OF CONTROL – GOTO

Many people have written at length about the unreadability of programs which contain arbitrary jumps. Most of their complaints are justified – you can write programs which no one, not even yourself, can understand if you make unrestricted use of gotos. There are, however, occasions when you find yourself driven to use them because none of the structured formats we have described so far will satisfy your needs. They can also be extremely useful when you find that you have discovered some new structured format that you would like to use. The POP-11 'macro' facility (described in Section 13.2) enables you to define such new formats. You will generally find that when you come to define such macros, you will make use of gotos.

The user can transfer control to a specified label by using the goto command. The label name is written immediately after the goto command, and is also written, with a following colon, at the point where control is to be transferred. For example:

```
define laugh();
    l: spr("ho");  ;;; Labelled command is print "ho" and a space
        goto l     ;;; go to label L and execute the associated command
enddefine;
```

If you call laugh, it will keep printing until you interrupt it.

Only labels inside the same procedure as the goto command can be accessed. Each label may only appear once inside each procedure, but there may be as many goto commands as you like for that label. gotos may jump either backwards or forwards.

POP-11's syntax is summarised in the Syntax Diagrams in the Appendix.

Exercises

1. Using a for loop, define a procedure, len, that takes a list as input, and returns the number of items in the list.

2. Write a procedure, trans, that given a number representing inches, produces a translation into feet and inches. This needs two output variables.

3. What is the difference between the following?

```
while <condition> do <action> endwhile
```

and

```
until <condition> do <action> enduntil
```

4. What would the equivalent of

```
vars num;
1 -> num;
while num * num < 100 do
    num + 1 -> num
endwhile;
```

be with an until loop?

5. If you wanted to print all the successive tails of [1 2 3 4], how would you do it using a for loop?

6. Using a for loop, define a procedure myrev, to behave like rev, which reverses the list given to it as argument.

7

Recursion

We have previously seen how new procedures can be defined in terms of old ones. Using display_room we defined display_data. Using the procedures pr, perim, area and volume, we defined display_room. Using arithmetic operations we defined the procedures perim, area and volume.

We can use procedures we have already defined to create yet more procedures, to form a 'procedural hierarchy'. For example, if we want to know the perimeter of a square, since its length and breadth are the same, we can use the previously defined perim to define square_perim:

```
define perim(len, breadth) -> result;
    (len + breadth) * 2 -> result
enddefine;
```

```
define square_perim(side) -> result;
    perim(side, side) -> result
enddefine;
```

We can call square_perim which, in turn, will call perim:

```
square_perim(3) =>
** 12
```

Procedures can make use not only of other procedure definitions. They can also make use of their own definition. This concept is known as 'recursion'. It is a very powerful technique. Anything that can be defined iteratively can also be defined recursively. It is often much easier, and makes more sense intuitively, to define something recursively than iteratively. It will not be explained yet, only illustrated.

Suppose that we have a list of words, and want to find out if a particular word is included. We might go about this by looking to see if the first word in the list is the word we want. If it is, we will stop looking, but if it is not, we will look at the second word in the list, and so on. We could write a procedure, called member, to test the first word in the list (that is, see if it is the same as the one we are looking for). If it is the word we want, member will return <true>. If it is not, we will then test the words in the tail of the list until either the word is found, or there are no more words to check (that is, we would apply member to the tail of the list). To define member in this way would be to define it recursively. Although member is intuitively pleasing, it is often clearer to introduce the mechanics of recursion using arithmetic examples.

For some kinds of statistical and algebraic calculations, we need to add up, or multiply, a sequence of numbers starting from 1 and going up to some target number. In 'desk-calculator mode', POP-11 can handle that:

```
1 + 2 + 3 + 4 + 5 + 6 =>
** 21
1 + 2 + 3 + 4 + 5 + 6 + 7 + 8 + 9 =>
** 45
```

What is the underlying pattern here?

An infinitely recursive procedure

Thinking of 6 as the 'target number', the first sequence could be described as:

(the sum of numbers up to one less than the target) + the target.

The same scheme also fits the second example. This could be translated into POP-11 as:

```
define sumup(target) -> result;
    sumup(target - 1) + target -> result
enddefine;
```

This is almost right but it fails to handle sumup(1) which we intend to be 1, but will actually come out as sumup(0) + 1; but sumup(0) is sumup(−1) + 0, and sumup(−1) is sumup(−2) + −1! There is an infinite regression here.

Stopping the recursion

To prevent such infinite regressions we need a stopping condition. In this case we want to stop the recursion when we get to 1, and to return 1 as the result when we get there. To encode that, we shall need to use a conditional statement saying that if the target number is 1, then 1 is the result, not sumup(1 − 1) + 1:

```
define sumup(target) -> result;
    if      target = 1
    then    1 -> result
    else    sumup(target - 1) + target -> result
    endif
enddefine;
```

We can now test sumup as follows:

```
sumup(1) =>
** 1
sumup(2) =>
** 3
sumup(5) =>
** 15
```

7.1 MAKING THINGS CLEARER WITH TRACE

We have seen that square_perim causes perim to run. This can be shown clearly if we use one of POP-11's powerful built-in debugging aids, trace. trace makes procedures print out information whenever they are invoked and whenever they finish. To trace perim and square_perim, we do:

```
trace perim, square_perim;
```

This alters the two procedures so that when they are invoked from now on, they print information saying when they start and stop, and show any arguments or results.

Suppose we now run square_perim:

```
square_perim(5) =>
>square_perim 5        ;;; starting SQUARE_PERIM with 5
!>perim 5 5            ;;; starting PERIM with 5 and 5
!<perim 20             ;;; PERIM finishes with result 20
<square_perim 20       ;;; so does SQUARE_PERIM
** 20
```

Procedures which have been traced print $>$, then their name, then their arguments when they are entered; and $<$, then their name, then their results (if any) when they exit. !$>$ means entering a procedure while already in a traced procedure. If we were inside two traced procedures we would get !!$>$, and so on. Similarly, !$<$ means leaving a procedure while already in a traced procedure.

To switch tracing off selectively you use untrace:

```
untrace perim;
square_perim(5) =>
>square_perim 5
<square_perim 20
** 20
```

Note that only perim has been untraced. square perim still reports what it is doing.

To switch off all tracing, do:

```
untrace;
```

Typing

```
trace;
```

will restore tracing of procedures not yet individually untraced.

We will make extensive use of trace to explain our examples from now on. We start by tracing sumup to illustrate how it calls itself recursively:

```
trace sumup;
```

Calling sumup now produces:

```
sumup(1) =>
>sumup 1          ;;; going into SUMUP with argument 1
<sumup 1          ;;; coming out with result 1
** 1


sumup(2) =>
>sumup 2
!>sumup 1
!<sumup 1
<sumup 3
** 3


sumup(5) =>
>sumup 5
!>sumup 4
!!>sumup 3
!!!>sumup 2
!!!!>sumup 1
!!!!<sumup 1
!!!<sumup 3
!!<sumup 6
!<sumup 10
<sumup 15
** 15
```

You can think of each invocation of sumup as a request to the computer to start obeying a new copy of the instructions in the definition. With each new copy come new values for the variables target and result. The old values of these local variables are remembered, since they may be needed after the recursive call returns. As it happens, the old value of result is not needed, since it is over-written by the assignment after the recursive call is completed, but the old value of target is. It is added to the result left on the stack by the recursive call. Without local variables, recursion like this would not work properly.

7.2 RECURSING ON A LIST OF LISTS

Recursing down a list of lists is a powerful technique. We start with a numerical example, which will be explained and traced, and follow it by a more complex non-numerical example. The procedure addup, below, adds up all the numbers in a nested list, no matter how deeply it is nested.

```
define addup(list) -> result;
    if list = [] then 0;     ;;; the stopping condition
    elseif islist(hd(list)) then
        addup(hd(list)) + addup(tl(list));
    else
        hd(list) + addup(tl(list));
    endif -> result;
enddefine;
```

In English this says, if the list has nothing in it, then 0 is the result. If the head of the list is a list, add up all the numbers this embedded list contains first, which may involve repeating the process, that is, recursively calling addup. When done, add up all the numbers in the tail of the list, which may also involve a recursive call of addup. If the head is not a list it must be a number, so a recursive call of addup is not required. In this case you just put this number on top of the stack ready to be added up at the end. Study the traced output with comments below:

```
trace addup;
addup([[1 2] 3 [4]])=>  ;;; calling ADDUP

>addup [[1 2] 3 [4]];;; entering ADDUP with list [[1 2] 3 [4]]
 !>addup [1 2]           ;;; hd(list) is a list, call ADDUP on this list
 !!>addup [2]            ;;; hd(list) not a list - call ADDUP on tl(list)
 !!!>addup []            ;;; for same reason call ADDUP on tl(list)
 !!!<addup 0             ;;; tl(list) = [], so exit that call with 0
 !!<addup 2              ;;; exit previous call of addup [2] with 2 + 0
 !<addup 3               ;;; exit addup [1 2] with 1 + 2
 !>addup [3 [4]]         ;;; call ADDUP on TL of original list
 !!>addup [[4]]          ;;; this time HD is a list so
 !!!>addup [4]           ;;; call ADDUP on HD of that list
 !!!!>addup []           ;;; hd(list) not a list, so call ADDUP on TL
 !!!!<addup 0            ;;; which is [] so exits with 0
 !!!<addup 4             ;;; exits addup [4] with 4 + 0
 !!!>addup []            ;;; stopping condition. List is now [] so
 !!!<addup 0             ;;; exits that call of ADDUP with 0
 !!<addup 4              ;;; exits addup([[4]]) with 4 + 0
 !<addup 7               ;;; exits addup([3 [4]]) with 3 + 4
<addup 10                ;;; exits addup([1 2] 3 [4]]) with 3 + 7
** 10                    ;;; prints the result from the stack
```

Non-numerical application of recursion

We have used arithmetical examples to illustrate recursion so far because of their relative simplicity. Recursion, however, is often most natural in non-arithmetic environments. It is widely used in work on language and thinking, and also in programs which perform perceptual tasks. A common non-numerical application of recursion is searching a tree or network, for example searching a family tree. The family tree example we now give works on the same principles as our hypothetical procedure member, outlined at the beginning of the chapter.

A simple example is searching through nested lists for a list starting with a given word. For example, here is a list of lists:

```
vars facts;
[[tom age 20 wife [mary age 30]]
 [suzy age 60 husband
         [joe nationality british father
                 [fred age 93 wife [sally age 94]]]]]] -> facts;
```

If you want to search such a list to see if it contains a list starting with the word "joe", you first look at the head of the list to see if it is "joe". If it is not, and if the head of the list is another list, then search that list. If you still do not find the word, then search the tail of the original list.

We need the built-in procedure atom to develop the program we want here. atom is a boolean procedure which returns <true> if given something other than a list with at least one element, for example a word or the empty list.

```
define search_for(target,list_of_lists) -> result;
    if atom(list_of_lists) then ;;; if input is [] or a word
        false -> result;      ;;; cannot find target in an atom.
    elseif hd(list_of_lists) = target then
        list_of_lists -> result
    else
        search_for(target, hd(list_of_lists)) -> result;
        ;;; if result is non-FALSE stop. If FALSE continue
        unless result then
            search_for(target, tl(list_of_lists)) -> result
        endunless;
    endif;
enddefine;
```

Notice the recursive calls of search_for, first on the head of list_of_lists, and then, if the first call produces a <false> result, on the tail. Below are examples of search_for looking for lists in the variable facts beginning with particular words:

```
search_for("fred", facts) ==>
** [fred age 93 wife [sally age 94]]

search_for("sally", facts) ==>
** [sally age 94]
```

Searching for something not in facts produces the following:

```
search_for("margaret", facts) ==>
** <false>
```

In the example below, we trace search_for to reveal what happens in the recursive activations. The output from trace is edited so that the essential structure of what is going on can be seen without being swamped by all the detail:

```
trace search_for;
search_for("joe", facts) =>
```

```
>search_for joe [[tom age 20 wife [mary age 30]]
               [suzy age 60 husband
               [joe nationality british father
               [fred age 93 wife [sally age 94]]]]]]

    ;;; this shows the search starting with the whole FACTS list.
    ;;; It is not the target, so look at the head of the list.

!>search_for joe [tom age 20 wife [mary age 30]]
!!>search_for joe tom
!!<search_for <false>

    ;;; no good, so keep going down the tail of the head
    ...    (;;; three dots show editing of the output of TRACE)

!!!!!!!!!!>search_for joe []     ;;; The empty list is an ATOM
!!!!!!!!!!<search_for <false>

    ;;; that completes the unsuccessful search down the
    ;;; head of facts. Now try the tail:
    ...
!>search_for joe [[suzy age 60 husband
                  [joe nationality british father
                  [fred age 93 wife [sally age 94]]]]]

    ...
!!!>search_for joe suzy
!!!<search_for <false>

    ;;; and so on, until
    ...
!!!!!!>search_for joe [[joe nationality british father
                       [fred age 93 wife
                       [sally age 94]]]]
!!!!!!!>search_for joe [joe nationality british father
                       [fred age 93 wife
                       [sally age 94]]]

    ;;; This succeeds, producing the list wanted, and the final
    ;;; result gets printed out:
    ...
** [joe nationality british father [fred age 93 wife
    [sally age 94]]]
```

All the programs we have seen so far are comparatively simple examples of recursive procedures. It is possible to have a large family of procedures which call one another recursively, but this will not be illustrated here in detail. A typical use of mutual recursion might be a grammatical analysis program. One of the procedures might recognise noun phrases, using a prepositional phrase recogniser to cope with noun phrases like 'the old man in the big room', where the prepositional phrase recogniser would use the noun phrase recogniser to cope with 'the big room'.

7.3 RECURSION AND LOCAL VARIABLES

An important thing to remember is that all input and output variables, for example target, list_of_lists and result, or any other variables declared within the procedure using vars, will be local to the procedure. This means that for each activation those variables may have different values, and they will not interfere with values assigned during other activations. This is because whenever a procedure starts to run, the values of any local variables it possesses are copied into a special part of the computer's memory. We have already discussed local variables in general. The same mechanism is used for saving and restoring the values of local variables for ordinary procedure calls and for recursive ones.

Exercises

1. Rewrite the definition of delete (see Chapter 6) recursively.
2. Using recursion, define a procedure, rec_rev, to behave like rev which reverses the list given to it as input.
3. Define a version of rev, called recursive_rev which reverses the order of elements in embedded lists as well as the order of the lists themselves. For example,

> recursive_rev([[tom brown] [mary green] [suzy white]]) =>
> ** [[white suzy] [green mary] [brown tom]]

The definition will be similar to addup, above.

8

The POP–11 matcher

8.1 MATCHES: AN INTRODUCTION

For many purposes it is useful to test whether some structured object, such as a list of words, fits a certain pattern. POP-11 has a built-in 'pattern matcher' which can be used for checking the correspondence of a list with a pattern. It is useful, for instance, for defining an interactive program whose responses depend upon the pattern of words typed in. The matcher also has many other uses.

The infix operator matches takes two arguments, both lists, and returns one result, a boolean. The first argument is called the 'datum', the second the 'pattern'. The datum is compared with the pattern. The pattern may contain special pattern elements, which are illustrated below. Notice the asymmetry: the pattern must be the second argument, never the first. To test a given list to see if it matches some specified pattern, we use the format:

```
<list> matches <pattern>
```

Matching is a powerful programming technique provided in some artificial intelligence programming languages, and used in many programs. We have already seen how the equality symbol = can be used to compare two lists. The operation matches provides more sophisticated facilities for matching lists against partially specified patterns.

8.2 THE NEED FOR THE MATCHER

The procedure delete, in Section 6.2.2, uses unless x = item to accomplish its aim.

```
define delete(item,list) -> result;
   vars x;
   [% for x in list do
        unless x = item then x /* left on stack */  endunless;
      endfor
   %] -> result
enddefine;
```

List representations of more complex situations do not exhibit their significant features in terms of single items considered in isolation. Rather, the norm is
one of a context, or co-occurrence, of elements. We are likely to want to know
whether a list contains two designated elements occurring in a particular order,
or even whether it satisfies some rather more complex condition. For example,
does the sentence start with a noun phrase? For now we shall consider only the
relatively simple cases. Suppose we have the list:

```
[a b c d e] -> x;
```

A relevant test might be to establish whether it contains b and d occurring in
that order. POP-11 provides a built-in procedure called member, like that described in Chapter 7. It takes an item and a list as input, and returns <true>
if the item is a member of the list. Otherwise it returns <false>. Doing

```
member("b",x) =>
** <true>
member("d", x) =>
**<true>
```

tells us that both are present, that is:

```
member("b", x) and member("d",x) =>
** <true>
```

However, we know nothing of their relative positions in x, nor indeed of their
intervening or surrounding context.

   We can capture this ordering of b and d by doing

```
x(1) = "b" and x(2) = "d"
```

which specifies that d should immediately follow b in the list. In fact the relationship that does obtain in x has the form:

```
x(2) = "b" and x(4) = "d"
```

   In this way we can specify any arbitrary patterning of elements in a list
structure. It will, however, be very tedious to try all possible combinations of
pairs of successive numbers. The situation gets even worse if you merely want to
test whether d occurs somewhere to the right of b, although you do not mind
where exactly.

8.3 DESCRIBING THE SHAPE OF A LIST PATTERN

The == (double equals) symbol in a pattern is used to denote any number of list elements, including no elements. Thus in the b, d example, the pattern for 'b immediately followed by d' would be:

```
[== b d ==]
```

'b followed somewhere by d' would be:

```
[== b == d ==]
```

All of the following lists meet this specification:

```
[a b c d e]
[b d]            ;;; remember that == matches NIL
[b a a c d f]
```

To test a given list, say x, for presence of this specified pattern, we would call matches like this:

```
x matches [== b == d ==] =>
** <true>
```

Exercise

1. What result would you expect from the following?

```
i.   x matches [a == e] =>
ii.  x matches [a == d == e] =>
```

== allows a lot of variation in x. This is often useful for representing generality, but is not always what we want. There are a number of ways in which we can tighten it up, when required. We might, for example, want just one intervening element between b and d. The = (equals) symbol in the pattern serves this purpose. Thus:

```
x matches [== b = d ==] =>
** <true>
```

The two symbols, == and =, are basic descriptors of pattern shape. We may think of them as 'gobbling up' intervening list items. We can call = 'gobble-one', and == 'gobble-any'. Two successive occurrences of = can represent two intervening list elements, as in [== b = = d ==]. However, since == matches any number of intervening elements, it makes no sense to have two successive occurrences of ==.

= and == help us characterise the linear shape of a pattern. We may also want to characterise its structural organisation. For example, we may want the first element in the target list to be a list itself. We will take the list building, from Section 5.1, again:

```
vars building dwelling;
[[shed house inn] barn hotel] -> building;
[shed house inn] -> dwelling;
```

To test if the head of building is a list, we can match building against the following pattern:

```
building matches [[==] barn ==] =>
** <true>
```

This device may be used to dig arbitrarily deep into a list structure.

The pattern, then, is a sort of picture, with lots of missing details, of the kind of list we are looking for.

8.4 USING VARIABLES IN A PATTERN SPECIFICATION

So far we have described our patterns in very literal terms by stating that there needs to be a b and a d, or a list. In practice the items we want to include in our specification may have been constructed by other procedures (and, as we shall see, by procedures that use matches). Typically, these items will be the values of variables. The following returns <false> because the first element of building is not the word "dwelling", but a list whose value is that of the variable dwelling:

```
building matches [dwelling barn ==] =>
** <false>
```

We need to enrich the pattern specification language so as to distinguish between words used literally, and words used as variable names. We do this with the up-arrow ^ prefix:

```
building matches [^dwelling barn ==] =>
** <true>
```

The use of the up-arrow in the pattern specification here is the same as that introduced in Section 5.3

The double up-arrow symbol, ^^, is used to splice a list into either the datum or the pattern. Thus

```
[^^dwelling barn hotel] matches [shed house inn barn ==] =>
** <true>
```

but:

```
[^dwelling barn hotel] matches [shed house inn barn ==] =>
** <false>
```

To illustrate the power of matches and the pattern language, compare the following definitions of the procedure element (which does the same job as the built-in procedure member):

```
define element(item, list) -> trueorfalse;
    if list = [] then
        false -> trueorfalse;
    elseif hd(list) = item then
        true -> trueorfalse;
    else
        element(item, tl(list)) -> trueorfalse
    endif
enddefine;

define element(item, list) -> trueorfalse;
   list matches [== ^item ==] -> trueorfalse
enddefine;
```

8.5 RETRIEVING DETAILS OF THE TARGET LIST

Often we do not merely want to see if something is recognised as fitting a pattern. We also want to get at the components of the list, and use them. We use the ? and ?? symbols to retrieve information. They are used more or less like = and == respectively, except that ? and ?? are followed by a variable name. The variable is later bound to the value of the matching element(s) in the datum. Read ?x as, set x to have as its value a single element in the matching target list. Read ??x as, set x to have as its value a list containing a sequence of elements in the matching target list. Hence, to set a variable, say p, to take on the value of a single list element, prefix the variable name with ?

```
[a b c d e] -> x;
vars p; x matches [== b ?p d ==] =>
** <true>
p=>
** c
```

Similarly, to set the variable to be some sequence of list elements use:

```
vars q; x matches [a ??q d ==] =>
** <true>
q=>
** [b c]
```

When the match fails because, for example, [a b c] does not match the pattern [?p ?q ?r ?s] , the queried variables may have their values altered as part of the matching process even though the overall match fails. The use of ? and ?? to extract portions of a list matching a pattern is sometimes referred to as 'pattern-directed structure decomposition'. It often makes programming much easier than having to use primitive low-level list-manipulating procedures like hd and tl.

Variables preceded by ?? are often referred to as 'segment variables', because they can match an arbitrary segment of the datum list. Note that ?? always assigns a list to the variable when the match succeeds. The following example gives list a new value, and then uses it:

```
[i like talking to you] matches [i ??list you] =>
** <true>

[you ^^list me?] =>
** [you like talking to me?]
```

This is typical of the sort of trick used by ELIZA (Weizenbaum, J. (1966), *ELIZA – A Computer Program for the Study of Natural Language Communication Between Man and Machine*. CACM 9:36–45).

8.6 THE MATCHER ARROW ––>

Sometimes you know the general form of a list, and you just want to access one or more specific elements. For instance, you may wish to dig out the first, or the last, element for some purpose. In cases like this, where we know in advance that the list will match a pattern, though we do not know all the details of the list, we just use the matcher to access components and assign them to variables. We use the operation ––> instead of matches to do this. The only difference between them is that matches produces a result, which it leaves on the stack, to be used, for example, in a conditional instruction. By contrast, ––> does not produce a result. It merely does the match. If, however, it cannot do the match (that is, if matches would have produced <false>) then ––> causes a mishap. Consider the following:

```
[1 2 3] --> [1 2 3] =>
**

vars x; [1 2 3] --> [1 ??x] =>
**

x =>
** [2 3]

[1 2 3] --> [3 2 1] =>
;;; MISHAP - NON MATCHING ARGUMENTS FOR -->
;;; INVOLVING:  [1 2 3] [3 2 1]
;;; DOING     :  --> compile nextitem compile
```

The first two uses of => do not print out any result, so we might just as well have used the semicolon to signal the end of the command. However, the match does work, and the second match gives x a value, just as matches would have. In the last case, the match fails, and a mishap results.

The simplest use of ––> is to check that a list has a certain format. For example

```
list --> [junction ==];
```

checks that list starts with the word 'junction'. If not, a mishap message is printed.

The operation —-> can also be used to decompose a list, that is, to assign some of its components to variables, as in:

```
vars first, second, rest; list --> [?first ?second ??rest];
```

This produces a mishap message if list has fewer than two elements (??x matches nil). Even if the match fails, the values of the queried variables may still be altered. If the match succeeds, first gets the first element as its value, second the second element, and rest a list containing all the remainder. Here is an example:

```
vars first, second, rest;
[mary had a little lamb] --> [?first ?second ??rest];

first =>
** mary

second =>
** had

rest =>
** [a little lamb]
```

Using —-> in a procedure

The procedure final, below, produces the last element of a list using the operation —->:

```
define final(l) -> result;
    l --> [== ?result]
enddefine;
```

Exercise

2.   Using the matcher arrow, write procedures to:

   (i) Return the head of a list

   (ii) Return the tail of a list

findroom revisited

We can illustrate the use of the matcher to simplify the definition of a searching procedure by redefining the procedure findroom introduced in Section 1.2, and defined there as:

```
define findroom(name, list_of_lists) -> data;
    ;;; search list_of_lists for one starting with name
    for data in list_of_lists do
        if data(1) = name then
            return();          ;;; i.e. stop the procedure
        endif;
    endfor;
    ;;; produce a mishap message
    mishap('ROOM NOT FOUND', [^name ^list_of_lists])
enddefine;
```

Compare this with the following:

```
define findroom(name, list) -> data;
    vars len, breadth, height;
    if list matches [ ==  [^name ?len ?breadth ?height] == ]
    then
        [^name ^len ^breadth ^height] -> data;
    else
        mishap('ROOM NOT FOUND', [^name ^list])
    endif
enddefine;
```

The line

```
if list matches [ == [^name ?len ?breadth ?height] == ]
```

runs matches with two inputs, namely the value of the variable list on the left and the pattern on the right. This tells the matcher what to look for in list. It says, look for any number of elements (matched against ==), then a list starting with the given name and containing three other things, followed by any number of elements (matched against == again).

Notice the difference between ? and ^ here. The searched-for information is represented by the list:

```
[^name ?len ?breadth ?height]
```

The symbol ^ says that the given name must be found. ^ can be read as 'use the value of', whereas ? can be read as 'set the value of'. That is, the three variables prefixed by ? will be given values depending on what numbers are found after name once the list with the name is found. If we had used ?name instead of ^name, then any name would have matched.

If matches returns <true>, the instruction after the then is obeyed. This ensures that the output local data has an appropriate value, which is returned as the result of the procedure.

If matches cannot find what is required in list, then it returns <false>, and the instruction after the else is obeyed, causing a mishap message to be printed out.

Using the fact that ––> produces a mishap message when a match fails, we could adopt the following even shorter definition of findroom:

```
define findroom(name, list) -> data;
    vars len, breadth, height;
    list --> [ == [^name ?len ?breadth ?height] == ];
    [^name ^len ^breadth ^height] -> data;
enddefine;
```

The versions of findroom using matches and ––> do not produce the original list of information, but a copy. Sometimes this is desirable, but sometimes it can be wasteful. A different organisation of the data, in which the name of the room is followed by an embedded list of measurements, would overcome this. Alternatively, findroom could use len, breadth and height as output variables, so that it returned three results without putting them into a new list.

8.7 RESTRICTED MATCHING

The basic concept of matching is that of an identity between some element, or elements, of the datum, and elements of the pattern. We can constrain this further by stating that an element in the datum have some specified property.

For example, in the ELIZA world the occurrence of a word indicating reference to the family (for example, son, father, mother, brother) in an input sentence, is an important response-determining cue. To detect set membership we can use a predicate, that is, a procedure which returns a boolean expression, as an affix to a queried variable in the pattern specification

```
vars x;
[my father loved me] matches [== ?x:family ==] =>
** <true>

[you remind me of my brother] matches [== ?x:family ==] =>
** <true>
```

where family is a (previously defined) procedure such as:

```
define family(word) -> result;
  member(word, [son father mother brother]) -> result
enddefine;
```

Restrictions using : can also control the matching of a ?? variable. In this case the predicate should be something which applies to a list.

If the : is followed by a number (not an expression which evaluates to a number, but an actual number) the item being matched is constrained to be something whose length is that number. This is normally used to constrain the lengths of segment variables, but it can also be used with ordinary pattern variables, and for checking the lengths of items which are not lists. For example:

```
[junction [lines l1 l2 l3]] matches [junction [lines ??lines:3]] =>
** <true>
lines =>
** [l1 l2 l3]

[junction [lines l1 l2]] matches [junction [lines ??lines:3]] =>
** <false>


[allan] matches [?word:5] =>
** <true>
word =>
** allan
[allan] matches [?word:4] =>
** <false>
word =>
** allan
```

In the last two examples, it is the length of the word "allan" which is being checked. Note that in the final example, word gets "allan" as its value even though eventually the match fails.

Exercise

3.   See if you can work out how to use matches to find the answers to the
exercises involving ^ and ^^ at the end of Chapter 5.

Table 8.1 summarises match notations.

Table 8.1 – A summary of match notations

Basic format:

list matches pattern

A pattern specification can contain:

(i)   [a b]
Literal words to be checked in the target list

(ii)   =
The 'gobble-one' spacer

(iii)   ==
The 'gobble-any' spacer

(iv)   ^a
Put into the pattern an object which is the value of the variable a.
That object will then be compared with the corresponding object
in the target list.

^(<expression>)
Put into the pattern whatever results from evaluation of the expression.

(v)   ^^a or ^^(<expression>)
The value of the variable or the expression must be a list. Put into the
pattern all the elements of the list, for comparison with elements of
the target list.

(iv)   ?a
Set a to have the value of a single element in the matching target list.

(vii)   ??a
Set a to have the value of a sequence of elements in the matching
target list.

(viii)   ?a:test
Only allow a to match an element such that test(a) is <true>

(ix)   ??a:test
Like (viii), but the test is applied to a sequence of elements from the
target list (as in vii).

Note that if the predicate test in (viii) and (ix) returns not <true>, but
some other non-false result, then the result will be assigned to the
variable a (rather than having the item that was matched assigned as
its value)

Note also that if test is a number, then the restriction on a is that its
length (as defined by the built-in procedure length) should be test).

8.8 A MORE SOPHISTICATED EXAMPLE

We end this discussion of the matcher by sketching how it might be used as the basis of a program for doing syntactic analysis of English. We are going to use it to define a number of procedures for recognising particular syntactic structures. We need first of all a database of words, and some procedures for recognising the type of each word:

```
vars words;
[[determiner    a the]
 [adjective     big red old]
 [noun          bus man]
 [verb          caught]] -> words;


define determiner(word);
    if      words matches [== [determiner == ^word ==] ==]
    then    [determiner ^word]
    else    false
    endif;
enddefine;


define adjective(word);
    if      words matches [== [adjective == ^word ==] ==]
    then    [adjective ^word]
    else    false
    endif;
enddefine;
```

and similarly for noun and verb. With these preliminaries done, we can define the rest of what we need:

```
define noun_phrase(text);
    vars d a n;
    if      text matches [?d:determiner ?n:noun ==]
    then    [NP ^d ^n]
    elseif  text matches [?d:determiner ?a:adjective ?n:noun ==].
    then    [NP ^d ^a ^n]
    else    false
    endif;
enddefine;


define verb_phrase(text);
    vars v NP;
    if      text matches [?v:verb ??NP:noun_phrase ==]
    then    [VP ^v ^NP]
    else    false
    endif;
enddefine;
```

```
define sentence(text);
    vars s p;
    if      text matches [??s:noun_phrase ??p:verb_phrase]
    then    [sentence ^s ^p]
    else    false
    endif;
enddefine;
```

```
sentence([the old man caught the bus]) ==>
** [sentence [NP [determiner the] [adjective old] [noun man]]
            [VP [verb caught] [NP [determiner the] [noun bus]]]]

sentence([the old man caught the big red bus]) ==>
** <false>
```

We will not go into the details of how this works, beyond pointing out that all the procedures used for restrictions return results other than <true> when they succeed. As a consequence, when they succeed their results are assigned as the values of the relevant variables. These variables can then be used for building up the next level of structure.

This is probably not the best way to write a natural language parser, but it is certainly the easiest way to get started. We end this chapter with an exercise to extend it to deal with more complicated forms of noun phrase.

Exercise

4. Alter the procedures for parsing noun phrases so that (i) they allow an indefinite sequence of adjectives between the determiner and the noun, and (ii) they allow noun phrases to include prepositional phrases, as in 'the man with the big nose' or 'the house on the hill'.

   See what your program does with the phrase 'the man on the hill with the telescope'.

The POP-11 database

9.1 MATCHING ON A CORPUS OF LISTS – THE DATABASE CONCEPT

The database package provides a simple mechanism for storing a collection of facts and retrieving them on a pattern matching basis. The database has many uses. For example, it can be used when writing programs for planning, vision, game playing and language processing. A very common use is to represent a situation, or a 'micro-world', by storing a collection of propositions about the world. Changes in the world can be represented by changes in the database.

The database is not some special sort of object. To POP-11 it is just another global variable. Its value is a list of lists. We may choose to interpret the database as a collection of facts, but POP-11 does not interpret the list at all; as far as POP-11 is concerned, the database is a list like any other list.

Various matching procedures work on the database, together with other standard procedures for manipulating this global variable. Some of these procedures can also be applied to other lists of lists.

This chapter introduces the procedures available for operating the database. The power of matching on the database is also illustrated. Using these techniques, we show how procedures in the rooms exercise (see Chapters 1 and 8) can be defined more easily and efficiently than before.

9.2 ADDING AND REMOVING DATABASE ITEMS

To see what the value of the database is, we do:

```
database =>
** [] ;;; the value is an empty list to start with
```

We can build up a database using the built-in procedure add. add takes one item as input and adds it to the database. For example:

```
add([room1 10 12 8]);
add([room2 6 11 8]);

database =>
** [[room2 6 11 8] [room1 10 12 8]]
```

Notice that items appear in reverse order to the order in which they were added.

We can add more than one item at a time more concisely by using the procedure alladd:

```
alladd([[room3 15 11 8] [room4 10 12 9]]);
database =>
** [[room4 10 12 9] [room3 15 11 8] [room2 6 11 8]
    [room1 10 12 8]]
```

Complementing add and alladd, we have remove and allremove:

```
remove([room3 15 11 8]);
database =>
** [[room4 10 12 9] [room2 6 11 8] [room1 10 12 8]]
```

The order of items in a call of allremove is not important. It does not have to reflect the ordering of the database. For example:

```
allremove([[room1 10 12 8] [room2 6 11 8] [room4 10 12 9]]);
```

remove takes one argument and searches through the database to find an instance of the argument. If it finds one, it removes it. If not, it generates a mishap. remove may be given a pattern as its input, that is, a partial specification of the item to be removed. It will remove at most one item, even if the pattern matches several. For example

```
remove([==]);
```

removes only the first item it finds in the database even though all items match the pattern. Similarly, allremove generates a mishap if it cannot remove something for each element of the list of patterns given to it as argument.

The procedure flush does not have these restrictions. flush takes one argument, a pattern, and removes all items in the database which match it. If there is nothing that matches, then flush does nothing. For example, with the database given above, the action

```
flush([==]);
```

clears the database:

```
database =>
** []
```

Thus flush([==]); is equivalent in this situation to:

```
allremove([[room1 10 12 8] [room2 6 11 8] [room3 15 11 8]
           [room4 10 12 9]]);
```

```
flush([==]);
```

empties the database no matter what is in it, and is therefore equivalent to:

```
[] -> database;
```

9.3 WHAT WAS REMOVED?

When you use flush or remove, the last item removed is stored as the value of
the variable it. For example:

```
add([room5 21 11 9]);
remove([room5 21 11 == ]); it =>
** [room5 21 11 9]
```

The procedure allremove uses the variable them instead. This will be a list of all
the items removed. add and alladd similarly use it and them respectively to record
what was added.

9.4 FINDING ITEMS IN THE DATABASE

The procedure present takes a pattern, and starts matching it against every database item. It returns <true> if a matching item is found, and <false> otherwise. For example:

```
alladd([[room1 10 12 8]
        [room2 6 11 8]
        [room3 15 11 8]
        [room4 10 12 9]
        [room5 21 11 9]]);

present([== 13]) =>
** <false>

present([== 8]) =>
** <true>
```

The variable it now holds whatever was matched:

```
it =>
** [room3 15 11 8]
```

present is frequently employed in conditional statements. For example:

```
if present(<pattern>) then <action> endif
```

Particularly common formats are:

```
if present(<pattern>) then
    remove(it);
    <do something with it>
endif;
```

and

```
while present(<pattern>) do
    remove(it);
    <do something with it>
endwhile;
```

In both these cases we look in the database for an object satisfying some condition. If we find one, we remove it from the database so that we do not find it next time we want to do the same thing, and then we do whatever it was we were interested in to it. The use of the variable it makes it very easy to do things like this.

foreach, explained below, provides a convenient format for doing something to each item in the database matching some pattern without removing the items after they have been found.

Example

We can illustrate the use of the database and present by redefining the procedure findroom:

```
define findroom(name) -> data;
    vars len breadth height;
    if present([^name ?len ?breadth ?height]) then
        [^name ^len ^breadth ^height] -> data;
    else
        mishap('ROOM NOT FOUND', [^name])
    endif
enddefine;

findroom("room1") =>
** [room1 10 12 8]
```

Note that the second input variable, list, in our previous definition of findroom, is not needed because we now use the global variable database as input. Alternatively, if we wanted to use findroom with different databases, we could use the heading

```
define findroom(name, database) -> data;
```

so that the database is localised within this procedure.

findroom can be defined more economically using it as the output local:

```
define findroom(name) -> it;
    unless present([^name = = =])
    then
        mishap('ROOM NOT FOUND', [^name])
    endunless
enddefine;
```

Retrieving values from within an item

Since all of the apparatus of matches is utilised in the above database procedures, present can be used to set values of appropriately queried variables in the pattern specification. For example:

```
database ==>
** [[room5 21 11 9]
    [room4 10 12 9]
    [room3 15 11 8]
    [room2 6 11 8]
    [room1 10 12 8]]

vars x;
present([?x == 8]) =>
** <true>
x =>
** room3
```

Notice that if you use ? or ?? before a word in a pattern, you should declare that word as a variable name — hence the vars x; above. If the variables in patterns are not declared locally to procedures which use them, then different procedures using the same variable names might change their value. This applies to procedures which use matches or any of the database operations.

lookup

We do not always want the matching item. Sometimes we know that the item is present in the database and just want the value of some fragment of it. The procedure lookup provides this facility. It does not return <true> or <false>, but merely sets the value of queried pattern variables when it finds an item matching its input argument. For example:

```
vars x;
lookup([room1 ?x ==]); x =>
** 10
```

If no match is found, it generates a mishap message:

```
lookup([room17 ?x ==]);
;;; MISHAP - LOOKUP FAILURE
;;; INVOLVING:  [room17 ? x ==]
;;; DOING    :  lookup compile nextitem compile
```

Just as we use ——> instead of matches when we know that the match will succeed, so we use lookup instead of present when we expect a database search to be successful. We can define findroom most economically as:

```
define findroom(name) -> it;
    lookup([^name = = =])
enddefine;
```

9.5 RETRIEVING ALL THE ITEMS PRESENT WHICH MATCH A PATTERN

There will often be a need to find not just one matching item in the database (or to set the value of queried pattern variables for just one matching item) but to find all of them. For this purpose the iterative construct foreach is provided. The general format of foreach is:

```
foreach <pattern> do <action> endforeach
```

For example, to print full information about every room in the database whose height is 8 feet, we can do:

```
foreach [== 8] do it => endforeach;

** [room3 15 11 8]
** [room2 6 11 8]
** [room1 10 12 8]
```

Note that foreach is a 'syntax' word (like if and define), not a procedure name, so the pattern specification that follows need not be enclosed in round brackets, ( ).

Inside the <action> the variable it is available to represent the database item which matches the pattern.

You can use the decorated list brackets, [%. . .%], to make a list of all the rooms with 8 foot ceilings:

```
vars sameceilings;
[% foreach [?x == 8]
    do      x
    endforeach %] -> sameceilings;

sameceilings =>
** [room3 room2 room1]
```

Each time round the loop, the value of x is left on the stack, and the decorated list brackets make a list of all of them.

foreach can be followed by in to specify a list other than database to search. The format is:

```
foreach <pattern> in <list> do <action> endforeach
```

9.6 CHECKING A SET OF PATTERNS AGAINST THE DATABASE

The procedure allpresent takes a list of patterns and tries to find a consistent way of matching the list of patterns against the database. In the process, pattern variables are bound. If a consistent match is found, allpresent returns <true> and assigns to the global variable them an instantiation of the lists of patterns (that is, it replaces variable names with their values). allpresent returns <false> if no consistent matches are found. For example, to find a grandson of tom we could do:

```
alladd([
       [dick father harry]
       [tom father jack]
       [bill father tom]
       [jack father dick]]);
```

```
vars x, y;
if allpresent([[tom father ?x] [?x father ?y]]) then y => endif;
** dick
them =>
** [[tom father jack] [jack father dick]]
```

In our rooms example, we could use allpresent to find a room whose length is the same as another room's breadth:

```
add([room6 11 21 9]);
database =>
** [[room6 11 21 9] [room5 21 11 9] [room4 10 12 9] [room3 15 11 8]
   [room2 6 11 8] [room1 10 12 8]]

vars a b p;
if allpresent([[?a ?p ==][?b = ?p =]]) then a=> b=> p=> endif;
** room6
** room5
** 11
```

The order of the items in the database, and the order of the patterns in the list of patterns, are both unimportant to allpresent. It may do its search more quickly if the patterns are provided in one order rather than another (in general, more highly specified patterns should be earlier in the list), but the final result will not be changed.

9.7 FOREVERY

forevery is to allpresent as foreach is to present. forevery allows some remarkably powerful manipulations of the database. Whereas allpresent finds just one way of matching a list of patterns against the database, forevery tries to find every possible way. We would use forevery, for example, to find all paternal grandfather relations, that is, all combinations of the form:

```
[?x father ?y] [?y father ?z]
```

Here is an example:

```
alladd([
      [dick father harry]
      [tom father jack]
      [bill father tom]
      [dick father mary]
      [jack father dick]]);

database ==>
** [[jack father dick]
    [dick father mary]
    [bill father tom]
    [tom father jack]
    [dick father harry]]
```

```
vars x, y, z;
forevery [[?x father ?y] [?y father ?z]] do
    [^x is the paternal grandfather of ^z] =>
endforevery;
** [jack is the paternal grandfather of mary]
** [jack is the paternal grandfather of harry]
** [bill is the paternal grandfather of jack]
** [tom is the paternal grandfather of dick]
```

Note that forevery makes sure that the value of y in the two patterns is the same. The permitted formats for forevery are:

```
forevery <list of patterns> do <actions> endforevery

forevery <list of patterns> in <list> do <actions> endforevery
```

When in <list> is omitted, the value of the variable database is used as the list to be searched for suitable combinations of items.

We could use forevery in our rooms example to find out which rooms are in between which. Suppose we added information about adjacent rooms to the database:

```
alladd([[room1 adjacent room2]
        [room2 adjacent room3]
        [room3 adjacent room4]
        [room4 adjacent room5]
        [room5 adjacent room6]]);
```

We could then do:

```
vars x y z;
forevery[[?x adjacent ?y][?y adjacent ?z]] do
        [^y is between ^x and ^z]=>
endforevery;

** [room5 is between room4 and room6]
** [room4 is between room3 and room5]
** [room3 is between room2 and room4]
** [room2 is between room1 and room3]
```

Exercises

1. What is present given as argument? What does it return as result? What would happen if we typed the following:

   ```
   if present([== a]) then => endif;
   ```

   Why? How could the problem be overcome?
2. How does foreach differ from present?

3. If we know that an item is present in the database, and want to find the value of some fragment of it, which database procedure would we use? How does it differ from present?
4. If you wanted to see if several patterns were present in the database, which procedure would you use? Which database variable would the matching items be assigned to?
5. How does forevery differ from allpresent?
6. Use the database to store information about direct family relationships, like [john father mary] [sue wife john] and so on. Then define procedures to interrogate the database to find out if x is the uncle of y, x is an ancestor of y, x is the great grandmother of y, etc.

10

Additional POP–11 data structures

We have seen plenty of examples of the commonly used data structures, formally introduced in Chapter 2, such as words, booleans, procedures and lists. In this chapter we introduce additional POP-11 data structures. We examine why, in certain circumstances, data structures such as vectors, strings, arrays, properties and dynamic lists provide a more compact and efficient data representation than ordinary lists. We also illustrate ways of constructing new data classes using the macros recordclass and vectorclass.

10.1 VECTORS

Vectors provide an alternative to lists as a way of storing collections of elements. They are very useful when it is important to save memory space or time to access arbitrary elements of the collection. A vector is a data structure made of some number of elements stored consecutively in the computer's memory. There are different types of vectors, including strings and standard vectors.

A 'standard' POP-11 vector may be created by writing its elements between curly brackets, {. . .}, just as square brackets are used for lists. Writing

```
{vectors are denoted by curly brackets}
```

creates a vector which is represented in memory as:

length	key	"vectors"	"are"	"denoted"	"by"	"curly"	"brackets"

Each box represents one word of memory. The 'length' box contains the number of items in the vector, in this case 6. The 'key' box points to an object of type **key** (see Section 10.3) which signifies that this is a standard vector. The other boxes contain pointers to the elements, in this case POP-11 words (see Chapter 2).

Lists, as shown in Section 5.2, are chains of items, where links in the chain, called pairs, may be located in very different places in the computer. A list of N elements requires N pairs. These take up 3N machine words, since each pair uses three words, the front, the key and the back, making 12N bytes on a VAX. A vector of N elements takes up N+2 words (the length and the key, plus a word for each element). Clearly, for large collections it is far more economical to represent them as vectors rather than lists. Lists are more flexible because links can easily be inserted or removed, but access can be slower. To find the 300th element of a list it is necessary for the computer to start with the first link and take 299 steps from link to link, whereas with a vector it can work out immediately how far from the beginning to jump to get the 300th element. The address can be computed from the initial address and the 'offset'. Fast access and reduced space are traded off against the inflexible structure.

List brackets and vector brackets may be combined to produce a list of vectors, or a vector of lists. Both sorts may be arbitrarily nested. Vector brackets, like list brackets, 'quote' their contents. That is, names of variables are not replaced by their values, and if there is a piece of enclosed POP-11 program, it is not executed. {99 + 9} is a vector containing two numbers and a word, not just one number. As with list expressions, if you want to use the value of a variable, or the result of some computation, you use the percent symbol or ^ or ^ ^ inside the brackets. For example:

```
[a b c] -> list; 3 -> x; 5 -> y;
{cat % hd(list), x + y, list %} =>
** {cat a 8 [a b c]}
```

Note that cat is outside the % signs, and hence is quoted. Note also that we can replace the use of % signs by the ^ symbol, just as for lists: {cat ^(hd(list)) ^(x + y) ^list}. The double up-arrow may be used for 'removing the brackets' from lists or vectors, as in:

```
{^^list } =>
** {a b c}

vars vector; {d e f} -> vector;
{a b c ^^vector g} =>
** {a b c d e f g}
```

10.1.1 initv

The procedure initv creates vectors. It takes a number as input and makes a vector the same length as the number. The elements are initially <undef> (see Chapter 2). For example:

```
vars v; initv(5) -> v;  ;;; create a vector of length 5
v =>
** {undef undef undef undef undef}
```

Vectors, like other data structures, can be compared using either = or ==.
The former returns <true> for two different vectors with the same elements.
The latter requires strict identity:

```
{a vector} = {a vector} =>
** <true>

{a vector} == {a vector}
** <false>
```

Note that although in many ways vectors are like lists, hd and tl cannot be
applied to them. ^, ^^ and matches can be used with vectors, but ? and ?? do
not work. matches works like = on vectors.

10.1.2 subscrv
An element of a vector may be accessed or updated using the procedure subscrv.
This takes two arguments, an integer and a vector. The integer specifies which
component to access. For example:

```
vars x; {a cat} -> x; subscrv(2, x) =>
** cat
```

To change the value of the second element, do:

```
"mouse" -> subscrv(2, x);  x =>
** {a mouse}
```

The second element of x has been altered by the 'updater' (see Chapter 11) of
subscrv. Altering structures in a program can sometimes lead to confusing
programs, but it is often very useful, for example in recording a changing situation.

Elements of vectors may also be accessed and updated simply by means
of a numerical index. For example:

```
x(2) =>
** mouse

"cat" -> x(2); x(2) =>
** cat
```

Vectors can be concatenated using <>. For example:

```
{a word} <> {and some more words} =>
** {a word and some more words}
```

10.2 STRINGS (Character vectors)

A string is a special kind of vector whose components are restricted to character codes between 0 and 255, that is, 8-bit integers (see Chapter 2). The structure of the string 'cat' is:

length	key	99	97	116

99 is the character code for 'c', 97 for 'a', and 116 for 't'. Each character in a string requires only eight bits of memory (a byte) rather than a whole 32-bit word like elements of a vector. The standard ASCII interpretation of integers as characters only uses the 7-bit numbers from 0 to 127. Different operating systems may do different things with integers between 128 and 255 when they are being treated as characters.

The quote marks, '...', may be used to create a string. For example, 'greetings' is a string containing the ASCII character codes for the letters in the word 'greetings'.

10.2.1 inits

The procedure inits creates strings. It takes a number as input, and makes a string the same length as the number. The elements of the string are initially set to the (8-bit) value 0. They cannot be set to <undef> because strings cannot contain pointers (see below). For example:

```
vars s; inits(3) -> s;  ;;; create a string of length 3
s(1) =>
** 0
```

Memory locations within strings each contain only 8 bits, so they cannot contain pointers, which require a full machine word. In a list or vector, a word of memory can contain only one object, which may be any POP-11 item, including a large number or pointer to another structure, so each field requires 32 bits of memory (on a 32-bit machine). A long string of 8-bit integers (between 0 and 255) uses about a quarter of the memory required for a vector containing the same integers. It uses about one-twelfth the space required for a list.

10.2.2 subscrs

The procedure subscrs accesses and updates elements in a string. It takes two arguments, an integer subscript and a string. For example:

```
vars s; 'cat' -> s;
subscrs(3, s) =>  ;;; print the third element of S.
** 116
```

To change the value of the third element of s, do:

```
100 -> subscrs(3, s);  ;;; 100 is the character code for "d"
s =>
** cad
```

A string cannot be given an element larger than 255:

```
500 -> subscrs(3, s);
;;; MISHAP - INTEGER 0 TO 255 NEEDED
;;; INVOLVING:   500
;;; DOING    :   subscrs compile
```

A string may be 'applied' to a number:

```
s(3) =>
** 100

112 -> s(3); s =>
** cap
```

Strings of characters, unlike words, are not stored in the dictionary, so the fact that two strings have the same characters does not make them the same string. POP-11 distinguishes the word quote symbol (") from the string quote ('):

```
vars string;
'A string with letters and spaces' -> string;

"cat" = 'cat' =>
** <false>
```

We saw in Chapter 2 that if you want to input a string which extends over several lines, the backslash, \, must appear at the end of each line. To input a string which will fit on one line, but print out on several, use the newline character, \n. For example:

```
'This is the first line \n and this is the second' =>
** This is the first line
 and this is the second
```

Similarly, \' inserts a string quote, \b inserts a back-space character, \t inserts a tab, \s inserts a space, and \r inserts the carriage return character.

To insert control codes into a string, use \^ before the capital letter, for example:

```
\^A    for <ctrl>A
\^B    for <ctrl>B
```

Other control codes can be inserted similarly, for example:

```
\^[    for <esc>
\^?    for <del>
```

Strings can be concatenated using the infix operations >< and <>, as shown below:

```
vars string1 string2 string3;
'1 2 3' -> string1;
' 4 5 6' -> string2;
string1 >< string2  -> string3;
```

```
string3 =>
** 1 2 3 4 5 6

'a string and ' <> 'another' -> string3;

string3 =>
** a string and another
```

The arguments of $><$ do not have to be strings. They can also be words or numbers, but the result will always be a string. So, if the value of x is an integer, to create a string made of the corresponding characters, concatenate it with the empty string thus:

```
x >< ''  -> numstring;
```

The difference between $<>$ and $><$ is that $<>$ is used for joining two objects of the same type to produce another object of the same type. $<>$ may be applied to a variety of data types, including procedures. $><$ is used for making strings out of other objects, such as words, numbers and lists. The two operations are equivalent when applied to two strings.

10.3 KEYS AND CLASSES

Every POP-11 data structure has in it a field containing a pointer to a 'key' structure. The key identifies the class of the structure (see Chapter 2.) For example, vectors contain a pointer to the vector key, procedures to the procedure key, keys to the key key and so on. The key associated with an object can be accessed using the procedure datakey:

```
datakey('asdf') =>
** <key string>
datakey([a list]) =>
** <key pair>
datakey(99) =>
** <key integer>
datakey("cat") =>
** <key word>
datakey(datakey('asdf')) =>
** <key key>
```

As well as identifying the class of any object to the system, keys also serve as a means of holding various items of information about that class, such as which procedure is used to print objects in the class, which procedure is to be used by the operation = in comparing them, and which procedures are used to manipulate fields in the structure.

We can define new classes of data with their own keys. A new class may be of type 'record' or type 'vector'. All records of the same class have a fixed number of distinct fields, possibly of different sizes, whereas vectors of the same class may have different numbers of fields, but all fields of a vector must be the same size. A pair is a record type, whereas vectors and strings are vector types. The built-in classes include other types which cannot be user-defined, for example booleans, keys, procedures and processes (see Chapter 14). conskey may be used to define a new data type by defining a new key for the type. Its format is:

```
conskey(<word>, <specifier>) -> key;
```

<word> becomes the dataword of the new class. <specifier> is either a field size, for a vector class, or a list of field sizes for a record class. A field size may be (i) the word "full" — meaning that the field can hold any item; (ii) a positive integer N specifying that the field can hold N-bit integers only; (iii) the word "decimal" or "ddecimal" indicating a low or high precision decimal number; (iv) a negative integer specifying a certain range of positive or negative integers. For example, for full vectors it would be 'full', for strings 8, and for pairs [full full] .

The key created automatically includes a constructor (like conspair or inits), a destructor (like destpair or deststring), and a recogniser (like ispair or isstring) for the new data class. In addition to these, a subscriptor and an initialiser are provided if the new data class is a vector class; accessors and updaters for all the specified fields are provided if it is a record class.

The two macros recordclass and vectorclass (see Chapter 12 for more on macros) provide convenient syntax for defining new classes of structures using conskey.

10.3.1 recordclass

recordclass is a macro for defining new record classes. A record class has a fixed number of distinct fields, which may have different field specifications. The format is:

```
        recordclass <classname> <field1> <field2> <field3> ...
```
or
```
        recordclass constant <classname> <field1> <field2> <field3> ...
```

where <classname> is a word to be the dataword of the class. The format of each <field> is:

```
    <fieldname> : <optional fieldspec>
```

If constant is included, then the identifiers declared by recordclass will be made constants (see Chapter 2). This protects them against re-declaration, and makes them more efficient.

<fieldspec> is an optional size specification, as explained for conskey. The default value is "full", that is, a full 32-bit word on a VAX. For example, a record class person can be defined as:

```
    recordclass person name age:7 sex;
```

People do not generally live beyond 128, which can be represented with 7 bits. We can create a new record, colin, by doing:

```
vars colin; consperson("colin", 15, "male") -> colin;
colin =>
** <person colin 15 male>
```

We can access information about colin by doing things like:

```
age(colin) =>
** 15
sex(colin)=>
** male
```

Trying to assign a number larger than 7 bits to the age field will produce a mishap.

The procedure birthday, below, adds one to the age field of a person and prints out a greeting. Note the use of string quotes and the concatenator, ><:

```
define birthday(person);
    age(person) + 1 -> age(person);
    'Happy birthday ' >< name(person) =>
    'You are now ' >< age(person) >< ' years old' =>
enddefine;
```

To call birthday on the record colin, do:

```
birthday(colin);
** Happy birthday colin
** You are now 16 years old
```

The procedure consperson, as explained above, is defined by the call of the macro recordclass. Also defined are the procedures destperson and isperson, and the accessors and updaters for each of the fields, name, age and sex.

```
destperson(colin) =>
** colin 15 male

isperson(colin) =>
** <true>

isperson("colin") =>      ;;; a word is not a person record
** <false>
```

10.3.2 vectorclass

vectorclass is a macro used to define new vector classes. It too uses conskey, and defines initialiser, constructor, destructor, subscriptor and recogniser procedures. Its format is:

```
        vectorclass <classname>  <optional fieldspec>
```
or
```
        vectorclass constant <classname>  <optional fieldspec>
```

<classname> will become the dataword of the class, and <fieldspec> (which defaults to "full") is the component size. Every component of a vector of the class must not exceed the size. If constant is present then the identifiers declared by vectorclass will be made constant. If strings were not yet in the system we could use vectorclass:

```
vectorclass mystring 8;
```

The <classname> is mystring. Each component of a mystring must fit into 8 bits of memory.

We make a data structure of type mystring in one of two ways. The first uses the constructor procedure, consmystring, which is defined by vectorclass. This takes an integer, and makes a mystring of that length from items on the stack. For example:

```
vars x; consmystring('h', 'e', 'l', 'l', 'o', 5) -> x;

x =>
** <mystring 104 101 108 108 111>
```

Alternatively, use the initialiser procedure initmystring produced by vectorclass. This takes an integer as argument and makes a mystring of that length, with elements initialised to 0 or <undef> depending on the fieldsize. For example:

```
vars w; initmystring(5) -> w;   w =>
** <mystring 0 0 0 0 0>
```

destmystring, also defined by vectorclass, puts the values of all the elements of a mystring on the stack, and returns the number of elements. For example:

```
destmystring(w) =>
** 0 0 0 0 0 5
```

vectorclass defines subscrmystring for accessing and updating elements in a mystring. For example:

```
3 -> subscrmystring(4, w); w =>
** <mystring 0 0 0 3 0>
```

We can also access or update the components of a mystring by using a numerical index to show which one we are interested in:

```
w(4) =>
** 3
66 -> w(2);  w =>
** <mystring 0 66 0 3 0>
```

The final procedure defined by vectorclass is the recogniser:

```
ismystring(w) =>
** <true>
```

If <fieldspec> is omitted, the default size is "full". So the following defines a vector class where each field occupies 32 bits.

```
vectorclass myvector;
```

10.4 ARRAYS

Arrays provide a way of storing information as if in a table of rows and columns. Two-dimensional arrays are often used for research in image processing. A three-dimensional scene might be represented by a 3-D array. POP-11 arrays may have arbitrarily many dimensions. An array of N dimensions requires N subscripts to access or update information. For example, items in a two-dimensional array are accessed by two integers, which may be thought of as representing a column and a row. A vector of length L can be thought of as a one-dimensional array, accessed by a single number between 1 and L. Array subscripts need not start from 1, or even from positive integers.

The elements of an array are stored in a vector, or vector type object (such as a vector of bits, or a string), called the 'arrayvector'.

There are two procedures available for making arrays, newarray and newanyarray. The difference is that the user can specify with newanyarray the type of data structure used to store the information. newarray always stores information in a 'full' vector. newanyarray is very intricate and not often needed.

10.4.1 newarray

The procedure newarray has two formats:

```
        newarray(<boundslist>) -> array;
and
        newarray(<boundslist>, <initialiser>) -> array;
```

$<$boundslist$>$ is a list of integers specifying the dimensions of the array. Each dimension has two integers specifying the lower and upper bounds for subscripts. Thus [1 10] indicates that we want a one-dimensional array, components numbered from one to ten, whereas [1 10 3 20] indicates that a two-dimensional array of 180 elements. [−5 5] determines a one-dimensional array with eleven components.

If $<$initialiser$>$ is omitted, the initial value of each array element is the word "undef". The second argument allows alternatives. It can either be a constant, such as [ ] to initialise every element in the array to be an empty list, or a procedure requiring as many arguments as there are array dimensions. If the latter, then the results of applying the procedure to every possible set of subscript values are stored in the array. So to create a 2-D array where the value at each field is the product of its subscripts (or co-ordinates) we can do:

```
define mult(a, b);
    a * b
enddefine;

vars myarray;
newarray([1 5 1 5], mult) -> myarray;
```

The first argument of myarray, the list [1 5 1 5], determines the dimensionality and subscript ranges of the array, and can be discovered using the procedure boundslist:

```
boundslist(myarray) =>
** [1 5 1 5]
```

The procedure mult is used to initialise the values in the array by multiplying combinations of subscripts. For example, the value of the element in row 4, column 3 is 12:

```
myarray(4, 3) =>
** 12
```

If there is no second argument, values default to <undef>:

```
vars non_init;
newarray([1 5 1 5]) -> non_init;
non_init(4, 3) =>
** undef
```

10.4.2 newanyarray
The procedure newanyarray takes between two and five arguments, as follows (where '/' represents alternatives):

```
newanyarray(<boundslist>,
            <initialiser>,
            <vector-type-spec/structure>,
            <access procedure/offset>,
            <mapping boolean>) -> array;
```

The two non-optional arguments are the <boundslist> and the <vector-type-spec> or <structure>. Permitted values are explained below.

The first two arguments are the same as for newarray, namely the <boundslist> and the optional <initialiser>.

The third, required, argument specifies which sort of data structure to store the elements of the array in. It determines the arrayvector of the array. There are three options for the third argument:

(i) a vector type key
(ii) a vector type object
(iii) a vector type initialiser procedure

(i) Vector type key
The 10 by 10 2-D character array blank, below, uses a string to store its components, initialised to the space character:

```
vars blank;
newanyarray([1 10 1 10], '\s', datakey('a string')) -> blank;
```

(ii) A vector type object, or an array
This allows the user to assign arbitrary initial values to the elements in the array. For example, an existing string of 'noughts and crosses' is represented by the array oxo, below:

```
vars oxo; newanyarray([1 3 1 3], '0 X X00 X') -> oxo;

oxo(1, 3) =>
** 79              ;;; the code for '0'
oxo(3, 3) =>
** 88              ;;; the code for 'X'
oxo(2, 1) =>
** 32              ;;; the code for a space
```

The elements of an array may be stored in another array, so that two different arrays can provide different views of the same data. For example:

```
vars array1; newarray([1 3 1 3], mult) -> array1;

vars array2;
newanyarray([1 3 1 3], array1) -> array2;

array1(2, 2) =>
** 4
array2(2, 2) =>
** 4
6 -> array1(2, 2);  array2(2, 2) =>
** 6
```

Here the arrayvector of array1 was used as the arrayvector of array2. When an array or vector is used to define the new arrayvector, its size must be consistent with the <boundslist> of the new vector. For instance, an array with <boundslist> [1 5 1 4] could be used for an array with <boundslist> [1 10 1 2]. If the structure supplied is too small a mishap results. It is acceptable for the vector to be larger than the bounds require. (More on this later.)

(iii) The third way to specify a type of arrayvector is to supply a vector type class-initiator procedure, such as initv or inits, for constructing vectors and strings respectively. If this option is used, then the fourth argument for newanyarray must be the appropriate subscriptor procedure such as subscrv or subscrs. A data structure of the minimum length needed for the array will be created. For example, the array multiply, below, creates a multiplication table, and uses initv to make a vector to store the elements in. The fourth argument is subscrv. This enables the accessing and updating the array:

```
vars multiply;
newanyarray([1 12 1 12], mult, initv, subscrv) -> multiply;
multiply(4, 3) =>
** 12
```

The fourth argument is a subscriptor, or an offset. As indicated, where the third argument is a class initiator procedure, the fourth must be the subscriptor procedure. If the third argument is an array or vector, the fourth may be an integer offset, indicating which portion of the vector or array supplied as third argument is to be used.

When applied to an array, the procedure arrayvector returns the (possibly shared) vector in which the array elements are stored. The procedure arrayvector_bounds returns the bounds of the portion of the vector used by the array. Normally, the bounds are 1 and the length of the vector, but not if an integer is provided as the fourth argument. Supplying this determines which element of the arrayvector the array is to count as its first. Thus, the elements of array1 are stored in a vector nine elements long, as shown by:

```
arrayvector(array1) =>
** {1 2 3 2 4 6 3 6 9}

vars lo, hi;
arrayvector_bounds(array1) -> lo -> hi;
lo, hi =>
** 1 9
```

Using an integer fourth argument we can force newanyarray to use only part of the vector supplied by the third argument. In the example below, the optional second argument is omitted. array3 is a 1-D array using only four elements in its nine element arrayvector. The integer 'fourth' argument says omit the first three elements of array1's arrayvector. The <boundslist> says use only the next four:

```
vars array3;
newanyarray([1 4], array1, 3) -> array3;
arrayvector(array3) =>
** {1 2 3 2 4 6 3 6 9}
arrayvector_bounds(array3) -> lo -> hi;
lo,hi =>
** 4 7

77 -> array3(1);
arrayvector(array3) =>
** {1 2 3 77 4 6 3 6 9}
array1(1,2) =>
** 77
```

The fifth argument is a boolean which is locally assigned to the variable poparray_by_row. It controls the mapping between subscripts and the vector the elements are stored in. The default value is <true>. For example:

```
vars row;
newanyarray([1 3 1 3], {a b c d e f g h i}) -> row;
row(3, 1) =>
** c
```

The mapping was arranged as follows:

3	g	h	i
2	d	e	f
1	a	b	c
	1	2	3

If <false> is assigned to poparray_by_row, the mapping takes place in columns. For example:

```
vars column;
newanyarray([1 3 1 3], {a b c d e f g h i}, false) -> column;
column(3, 1) =>
** g
```

The mapping took place as follows:

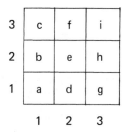

10.5 PROPERTIES

A property is a table of associations between objects. It functions as a kind of memory of what goes with what. It is a table of item—value associations. We can, for example, define a property called opposite consisting of pairs of items representing opposite directions, such as north and south, and east and west. We can then use the property opposite as a procedure. If we ask for opposite("north"), it will return "south". There are two procedures available for creating properties, newproperty and newassoc.

10.5.1 newproperty
The procedure newproperty takes four arguments. Its format is:

```
newproperty(<list>, <num>, <val>, <bool>) -> property;
```

<list> is a list of the initial item—value associations. This can be nil.

<num> is an integer specifying the size of the table.

<val> is the default value for any item not in the table.

<bool> is a boolean value. If it is the item <true>, the property is permanent. If it is <false>, the property is temporary. This means that if all pointers to an item—value association are lost, if the property is permanent, then the pair will not be reclaimed by the system's storage manager.

Example
We can create the property opposite as follows:

```
vars opposite; newproperty([], 100, false, true) -> opposite;
```

There are no item–value associations to begin with. The size of the table is 100 (see below). The default value returned for items not in the table is <false>. The property is permanent. To add an association, we do:

```
"south" -> opposite("north"); opposite("north") =>
** south
```

The default value is <false>, as shown by:

```
opposite("east") =>
** <false>
```

We could have provided the item–value associations when we created the table, by supplying them in a list. For example:

```
newproperty([[north south][south north][east west][west east]],
                           100, false, true) -> opposite;
```

newproperty produces properties in a 'hashed' association table. That is, it stores item–value associations according to their hash code. A hash code is a number derived from the address of the item. For example, if the address of "north", above, is 1,457,876, the hash code might be just the last two digits, 76. A vector is used to store the chains of item–value associations in the property. If the vector is 100 elements long (as defined by the second argument to new-property) the 76th element will contain the item north and the value associated with it. If the address of a different item is 1,242,376, that will also be accessed via the 76th element of the vector. In this case, the appropriate matching value of the item will have to be searched for through a list of items which all appear at the same position. Though large tables take up more memory space, they can be searched more quickly than smaller tables since the likelihood of items sharing a hash code diminishes. The size of the table is not a limit on the number of associations that may be stored; it is a count of how many items may be stored individually, rather than appearing in lists with other items which share the same hash code.

10.5.2 newassoc

The procedure newassoc makes properties in exactly the same way as newproperty, but the user only has to provide one input argument, the item–value list. Its format is:

```
vars prop; newassoc([]) -> prop;
```

The other three arguments used in newproperty are provided by default. The size of the table in which to store the property is 20, the default value for items not in the table is <false>, and the property is permanent. Using newassoc, we can define the property opposite as:

```
vars opposite; newassoc([]) -> opposite;
```

We can add item–value associations by doing:

```
"south" -> opposite("north"); opposite("north") =>
** south
```

We can also initially provide the item—value associations in a list:

```
newassoc([[north south][south north][east west][west east]])
                                           -> opposite;
```

10.5.3 appproperty

To do something to every item—value association in the property table, for example, print them out, we can use the procedure, appproperty. appproperty takes two arguments, a property and a procedure. The procedure takes two arguments, one to correspond to an item, the other to correspond to its associated value. The procedure print_opposites, below, prints out all the association pairs in the property opposite. The arguments to appproperty are the property opposite, and the procedure printout, also defined below:

```
define printout(item, value);
    [the opposite direction to ^item is ^value] =>
enddefine;

define print_opposites;
    appproperty(opposite, printout);
enddefine;
```

We call print_opposites thus:

```
print_opposites();
** [the opposite direction to south is north]
** [the opposite direction to east is west]
** [the opposite direction to west is east]
** [the opposite direction to north is south]
```

10.6 DYNAMIC LISTS

Lists in POP-11 can be dynamic. A dynamic list is one that is expanded only as it is required, which saves space and time. It may be infinitely long, and may contain elements not known about when the list was constructed.

Dynamic lists are constructed, like ordinary lists, out of chains of pair cells. Where the last pair cell in an ordinary list contains a pointer to the empty list, nil, the final pair in a dynamic list contains another pair whose front is <true>, and whose back is a procedure. This procedure will generate the next item in the list when it is called.

Dynamic lists are created with the procedure pdtolist. This takes a procedure as argument, and creates a dynamic list whose elements are the items produced by successive calls of the procedure. Accessing the head or tail of the dynamic list causes the procedure to be called. The procedure must be a generator so that it produces either the element to be the next item in the list, or <termin> if there are no more to come. The result is added to the end of the list by putting it in the front of the special pair, and constructing another special pair to go in its back. The old dynamic pair thus becomes the last proper pair of the list.

Example

The procedure gensym takes a 'root-word' as input, and outputs the word with a numerical suffix. Each time gensym is called, it increments the suffix by one. For example:

```
repeat 4 times gensym("day") endrepeat =>
** day1 day2 day3 day4
```

A number can be assigned to the suffix by doing:

```
7 -> gensym("day"); gensym("day") =>
** day7
```

Calling the procedure gencat, below, has the same effect as calling gensym("cat");:

```
define gencat();
     gensym("cat");
enddefine;
```

We can create a dynamic list, catlist, whose front is <true>, and whose back is the procedure gencat, with the following:

```
vars catlist; pdtolist(gencat) -> catlist;
```

The special pair, catlist, can be represented as:

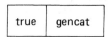

catlist is an unexpanded dynamic list, as can be seen if you do:

```
catlist=>
** [...]     ;;; the dots represent the dynamic part of the list
```

Asking for the head of catlist causes the procedure in the back of catlist to be applied. Tracing gensym makes the output clearer:

```
trace gensym; hd(catlist) =>
>gensym cat
<gensym cat1
** cat1
```

Accessing the head of catlist causes gencat to be called. This produces cat1. cat1 is put in the front of the special pair, and a new special pair is constructed to go in its back. catlist becomes a list with cat1 at the front, and a dynamic list at the back. The effect of the operation can be represented as follows:

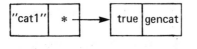

```
catlist =>
** [cat1 ...]     ;;; the dots represent the dynamic list.
```

catlist is an infinitely long list. It is only expanded as the user requires. Asking for the fourth element of catlist causes gencat to be called until there are four elements:

```
catlist(4) =>   ;;; automatically expands CATLIST to be 4 long
>gensym cat
<gensym cat2
>gensym cat
<gensym cat3
>gensym cat
<gensym cat4
** cat4

catlist =>
** [cat1 cat2 cat3 cat4 ...]
```

cat1, cat2, cat3, and cat4 form an ordinary chain of pairs in catlist. If we ask for the third element of catlist, gencat is not called, since catlist has already been expanded to contain more than three elements:

```
catlist(3) =>    ;;; third element of CATLIST is:
** cat3
```

The fourth tail of catlist is the dynamic list. If we assign this to catlist, it once again becomes unexpanded:

```
tl(tl(tl(tl(catlist)))) -> catlist;
catlist =>
** [...]
```

Exercises
1. Make the value of vec a vector containing the words in:
    'this is a vector'. Show two different ways of replacing the word 'this' by the word 'what'.
2. If we defined mystring, as above, and then did

    ```
    vars y;
    consmystring('y', 'e', 2) -> y;
    ```

    what would be the result of doing:

    ```
    y =>
    ```

3. Define a record class, called route, to enable you to store the following information:

    (i) The A23 goes from London to Brighton. The distance is 50 miles, the direction is north.

(ii) The A27 goes from Brighton to Lewes. The distance is 8 miles, the direction is east.

(iii) The A26 goes from Lewes to Tunbridge Wells. The distance is 25 miles, the direction is north-east.

The following should be possible:

```
distance(London_Brighton) =>
** 50

direction(London_Brighton) =>
** north

road(Lewes_T_Wells) =>
** A26
```

4. (i) How many dimensions does the array myarray, below, have?
   (ii) What are the lower and upper bounds for the dimensions?
   (iii) At least how many words of memory will the vector that houses myarray have to have?

```
vars myarray;
newarray([1 4 1 6]) -> myarray;
```

5.
```
vars vec_array;
newanyarray([1 3 1 3], initv(15), 5) -> vec_array;
```

   (i) What does the arrayvector of vec_array look like?
   (ii) What are the arrayvector bounds of vec_array?

6. Correct the following:

```
vars bad_array;
newanyarray([1 5 3 6], mult, inits, false) -> bad_array;
```

7. Write a procedure, printarray, that prints the array elements in columns and rows. For example, the command

```
printarray(array1);
```

   should print array1 (from Section 10.4.2) as follows:

```
1   2   3
2   4   6
3   6   9
```

8. Define newassoc. Hint, it is defined using newproperty.

9. Using appproperty, define a procedure to count how many item—value associations are in the property opposite.

10. What is the difference between a dynamic and an ordinary list? What is the advantage of dynamic lists?

11. What do you think the following will produce?

```
length(catlist) =>
```

11

Procedures revisited

We have explained quite a lot about how procedures are defined and how they may be called. Procedures in POP-11 are data structures, and as such they have various sub-components which may be accessed and updated by other bits of your program. This chapter discusses some of these fields, and also introduces some new techniques for making use of procedures. We will introduce even more ways of using them in Chapter 14.

We begin this chapter by describing the pdprops and updater fields. The system makes use of the pdprops field when printing, and the updater field when changing a value in a data structure. We then illustrate an important POP-11 facility, partial application. Finally, we demonstrate the reverse Polish notation for procedure calls in POP-11.

11.1 pdprops

When a procedure is defined, the name is assigned to the pdprops field (pdprops is a contraction of 'procedure properties'. Several of the procedures associated with procedure records begin with the letters pd). The pdprops is used by the error handler when it wants to print out details of the calling sequence, so it normally contains the name of the procedure. You can associate arbitrary data with your procedures by assigning it to their pdprops. This will clearly interfere with the way the error handler uses the pdprops, but you may be prepared to put up with that. (For example, if you wanted to keep a pointer to the definition of the procedure for debugging purposes, you might keep it in the pdprops.) We will not go into details about using the pdprops for anything other than the name of the procedure, as in:

```
define greet(name);
    [hello ^name] =>
enddefine;

pdprops(greet) =>
** greet
```

The system makes use of the pdprops of a procedure when printing. For example:

```
greet =>
** <procedure greet>
```

The user can assign anything to the pdprops of a non-system procedure. For example:

```
"friendly" -> pdprops(greet); pdprops(greet) =>
** friendly

vars t; greet -> t; pdprops(t) =>
** friendly
```

When a mishap occurs, the system normally prints out, on the DOING line, the pdprops of all the procedures that are currently being executed. The only exceptions are those procedures whose pdprops are <false> or words beginning with 'sys . . .'. For example:

```
define secondgreet(list);    ;;; GREET takes the second element
    greet(hd(tl(list)))      ;;; of LIST as argument
enddefine;

secondgreet([julia]);

;;; MISHAP - NON-EMPTY LIST NEEDED
;;; INVOLVING:  []
;;; DOING    :  hd secondgreet compile nextitem compile
```

11.2 updater

We have met the term 'updater' several times already. For example, the procedures subscrs and subscrv (see Sections 10.1.2 and 10.2.2) can change the components of their respective data structures by calling the updater part of their definitions. Below, we illustrate the updater of the procedure hd, and then show you how to define your own updaters. For example, if we have the list

```
vars x;
[1 2 3 4] -> x;
```

the command

```
hd(x) =>
** 1
```

accesses the first element of x. The command

```
5 -> hd(x);
```

updates the first element of x, as shown when we do:

```
x =>
** [5 2 3 4]
```

When POP-11 sees a procedure call on the right-hand side of the assignment arrow, as in

```
5 -> hd(x)
```

it uses the updater of that procedure. The updater of most procedures is <false>; attempting to use such procedures in update mode will cause a mishap. For example:

```
define second(list);
    hd(tl(list));  ;;; accesses the second element of a list
enddefine;

updater(second) =>     ;;; find out the value of the updater
** <false>

7 -> second(list);    ;;; MISHAP caused by <false> updater:

;;; MISHAP - EXECUTING NON-EXISTENT UPDATER
;;; INVOLVING: <procedure second>
;;; DOING    :  compile nextitem compile
```

By giving the updater of second a value, for example, the procedure setsecond, defined below, imperatives such as

```
7 -> second(list);
```

become legal. For example:

```
define setsecond(item, list);
    item -> hd(tl(list))
enddefine;
```

setsecond changes the second element of list. This is legitimate because hd has an updater. If we assign the procedure setsecond to be the updater of second,

```
setsecond -> updater(second);
```

we can now do:

```
vars x; [1 2 3 4] -> x;

7 -> second(x); x =>
** [1 7 3 4]

10 -> second(x); x =>
** [1 10 3 4]
```

A more convenient syntax for declaring updaters is illustrated by:

```
define updaterof second(newval, list);
    newval -> hd(tl(list)) ;;; HD has an updater
enddefine;

7 -> second(x); x =>
** [1 7 3 4]
```

The word updaterof in the definition indicates that we are defining the updater of second, not second itself. The first argument of any procedure being used as an updater is the item that will appear on the left-hand side of the assignment arrow. The updaterof syntax may be used even if the procedure that is being given the updater does not yet exist.

11.3 PARTIAL APPLICATION

Partial application allows specialised versions of general procedures to be defined. For example, suppose we want to define a predicate called iscolour that returned <true> if its argument was a colour, and <false> if not, a specialised version of member, recognising only colours, would be ideal. Partial application allows us to restrict a procedure's input in this way. First, here is how member might be defined:

```
define member(item, list);
    if list = [] then
        false
    elseif item = hd(list) then
        true
    else
        member(item,tl(list))
    endif
enddefine;
```

11.3.1 partapply

The procedure partapply is used for partial application. partapply takes two arguments, a procedure and a list. Its result is a new procedure, called a 'closure', based upon the given procedure. Its format is:

```
partapply(<procedure>, <list>) -> closure;
```

The closure requires fewer arguments than the original procedure, the rightmost of the arguments of the given procedure being supplied by the values in the list when partapply was called. If the procedure being partially applied has an up-dater, then the resulting closure will have an appropriate updater too. Using partapply, iscolour can be defined thus:

```
vars iscolour;
partapply(member, [[red blue green grey]]) -> iscolour;

iscolour("red") =>
** <true>
iscolour("elephant") =>
** <false>
```

member is being partially applied to the list [red blue green grey] and the result is assigned to the procedure iscolour. iscolour is a 'closure' of member, where the second argument of member has the list [red blue green grey] as its 'frozen' value. Note that iscolour has fewer input arguments than member.

In POP-11, the percent symbol, %, can be used to denote partial application more concisely. Using this notation, iscolour can be expressed as:

```
vars iscolour; member(%[red blue green grey]%) -> iscolour;
```

The procedure findone, below, takes two arguments, a list and a predicate. It prints any items in the list for which the predicate returns <true>:

```
define findone(list, predicate);
    unless  list = [] do
        if       predicate(hd(list))
        then     hd(list) =>
        return();
        endif;
        findone(tl(list), predicate)
    endunless;
enddefine;

findone([3 donkey [list]], islist);
** [list]

findone([chair house cat grey], iscolour);
** grey
```

By simply defining different closures of findone, we can produce specialised selection procedures. The examples below illustrate procedures to print colours and words.
getcolour is a closure made by partially applying findone to the closure iscolour:

```
vars getcolour; findone(%iscolour%) -> getcolour;

getcolour([apple red house]);
** red
```

getword is a closure made by partially applying findone to the predicate isword:

```
vars getword; findone(% isword %) -> getword;

getword([[list] 'string' {vector} 4 word]);
** word
```

Making closures of findone is more economical than defining each of the above procedures separately. It also allows the general version of findone to be extended, perhaps to do some extra error checking, and the extension would apply to all the closures produced from it (after they have been recreated).

Partial application is a powerful tool for creating 'super-procedures' which can be specialised to form different procedures. This often aids modular program design as well as saving space.

11.3.2 frozval

The procedure frozval (and its updater) accesses the arguments frozen into closures. It takes two arguments — a number, specifying which frozen argument (numbering from the left) is to be accessed, and the closure. For example:

```
frozval(1, iscolour)=>
** [red green blue grey]

frozval(2, iscolour)=>
;;; MISHAP - FROZVAL NUMBER OUT OF RANGE
;;; INVOLVING:  2 <procedure member>
;;; DOING    :  frozval compile nextitem compile
```

The mishap is caused because there is only one argument frozen into the closure iscolour. Any number of arguments may be frozen into a closure.

To add 'mauve' to the list of colours frozen into the closure iscolour, we could do:

```
"mauve" :: frozval(1,iscolour) -> frozval(1,iscolour);

frozval(1, iscolour)=>
** [mauve red green blue grey]
```

If the closure is itself based upon a closure, frozval accesses the arguments frozen into the top level closure. For example:

```
frozval(1, getcolour) =>
** <procedure member>
```

Note that the object frozval finds is printed out misleadingly. frozval finds that the frozen value is iscolour. iscolour cannot be printed out as such since it is a closure whose pdprops are <false>. When this is the case, the printer shows the pdprops of the pdpart (see below). We can see that it was in fact iscolour that was found by doing:

```
frozval(1, getcolour) = iscolour =>
** <true>
```

11.3.3 pdpart

The procedure pdpart takes a closure as argument, and returns the procedure upon which the closure is based. For example:

```
pdpart(iscolour)=>
** <procedure member>
```

If the closure itself is based upon a closure, only the pdpart of the top level closure is accessed. For example:

```
pdpart(getcolour)=>
** <procedure findone>
```

pdpart also has an updater, so you can do rather bizarre things like changing the procedure which is to be applied to the frozen arguments. This is not something which you will want to do very often.

datalist

We saw in Chapter 5 how the procedure datalist returns a list of the components of the object given to it as argument. datalist can also be applied to closures. In this case, datalist returns a list of all the arguments frozen into that closure, unlike frozval which returns just one. For example:

```
datalist(iscolour) =>
** [[red green blue grey]]
```

A further example

Using partial application, we can define a simple procedure for tracing other procedures. The procedure announce, below, is the general procedure:

```
define announce(proc);
    [^(pdprops(proc)) called] =>;
    proc();
    [^(pdprops(proc)) finished] =>;
enddefine;
```

To get some of the effect of the POP-11 trace mechanism, we can alter any procedure by partially applying announce to it. For example, addup, below, puts the sum of a list of numbers on the stack:

```
define addup(list) -> r;
    if list = [] then 0 -> r;
    else hd(list) + addup(tl(list)) -> r;
    endif
enddefine;

addup([1 2 3]) =>
** 6
```

To partially apply announce to addup we do:

```
announce(%addup%) -> addup;
```

addup is now altered so that it announces when it is called and left, for example:

```
addup([1 2 3])=>
** [addup called]
** [addup called]
** [addup called]
** [addup called] ;;; ADDUP is recursive, hence the four calls
** [addup finished]
** [addup finished]
** [addup finished]
** [addup finished]
** 6
```

The system procedure trace is more informative since it prints the successive arguments given to addup.

To unannounce addup, we retrieve the value frozen into the closure addup, and assign it to addup, for example:

```
frozval(1, addup)=>
** <procedure addup>

frozval(1, addup) -> addup;
addup([1 2 3]) =>
** 6
```

We could define a procedure for altering other procedures so they announced themselves as follows:

```
define set_announce (proc);
    announce(% valof(proc) %) -> valof(proc);
enddefine;
```

set_announce is given a procedure name. It gets the procedure itself, using valof, and makes a new procedure out of it by wrapping announce round it, just as we did above for addup. Finally, it makes this new procedure the value of the name, so that next time the procedure is called the new version gets used. This is very similar to the way the standard trace package operates, except that trace is defined as a 'macro' (see Section 13.2.1).

11.4 REVERSE POLISH NOTATION

POP-11 permits an alternative notation for procedure calls. Instead of

```
perim(3, 5) =>
```

you can use

```
3, 5 .perim =>
```

which can be interpreted as, put 3 and 5 on the stack, and then run perim. Nested procedure calls are written with this notation by writing them in the reverse of the usual order, so that

```
sin(sqrt(100)) =>
```

can be expressed as:

```
100.sqrt.sin =>
** 0.173648
```

The latter notation corresponds more closely to the actual order of processing, though the former is the more conventional way of representing procedure calls. Although we do not use the reverse Polish notation here, it is popular with some POP-11 users. It is quite often used for distinguishing between procedure calls you are trying out, and ones that you are using to print out the results, as in:

```
sqrt(arctan(sin(55))); .pr;      ;;; Do the sum, print the results
```

Exercises
1. How can

```
partapply(findone, [^iscolour]) -> getcolour;
```

be expressed using the % notation?
2. Define an updater for iscolour so that imperatives such as

```
true -> iscolour("red");
false -> iscolour("white");
```

become legal.

Hint: if a colour is to be added to the list of colours frozen in as argument to the procedure iscolour, append the colour onto the front of the frozen value of iscolour. If the colour is to be deleted, remove it from the frozen values.

12

Input/output

The basic procedures needed for controlling input and output (I/O) are introduced in this chapter. These procedures may be used by the compiler, which must know where to retrieve characters from and send characters to, or by user procedures which are required to read in or print out data. Things that are read in are referred to as the 'input'. The source for input characters is usually the terminal keyboard or a disc file.

The term 'output' can be ambiguous, meaning either things that are printed out on some device such as a terminal screen or a disc file, or results produced by procedures. In this chapter we are concerned with 'output' in the sense of characters which are sent to a device. Output is usually directed to a disc file or the terminal screen, but may go to some other peripheral device, such as a robot arm.

When we have explained how to do input and output to and from the terminal, we go on to how you can write programs to retrieve and send characters to different places. The user can also alter output produced by the POP-11 printing procedures such as pr and =>. How to determine where and how items are printed is illustrated. The differences between character input and output in raw and non-raw mode is also explained.

POP-11 provides a number of low-level procedures including syscreate, sysopen, sysclose, sysread, syswrite, sysflush and others for accessing terminals, disc files, 'pipes' and other devices. These will not be described in this book. Readers with access to POPLOG may consult the ref sysio file for details.

12.1 CHARACTER REPEATERS

Most input in POP-11 proceeds via a character repeater, that is, a procedure which reads characters one at a time from a file or the terminal. A character repeater puts what it has read onto the stack. It takes no arguments.

12.1.1 charin

charin is a character repeater that reads a character from the terminal, that is, from key presses. In POP-11, characters are represented as ASCII codes, which are integers between 0 and 127. For example:

```
charin() =>
t
** 116
```

12.1.2 discin

The procedure discin produces a character repeater for reading characters from a file. It takes the name of the file that the characters are to be read from as input, and returns a character repeater. The user assigns the character repeater to a variable, as in:

```
discin(<filename>) -> repeater;
```

Each time the character repeater held in repeater is called, it reads another character from <filename> and puts it on the stack. For example

```
vars charrep;
discin('fromfile') -> charrep;
```

produces the character repeater charrep, which reads characters from the file fromfile one at a time. Suppose fromfile contained the following text:

```
[the cat sat on the mat]
```

If we do

```
repeat 10 times charrep() => endrepeat;
```

the first 10 characters read from the file fromfile by charrep are printed out on the terminal screen:

```
** 91
** 116
** 104
** 101
** 32
** 99
** 97
** 116
** 32
** 115
```

12.2 termin

The identifier termin holds a special item used by character repeaters and item repeaters. A character repeater returns <termin> (which is the value of termin), as opposed to a character code, to indicate the end of the input. It is the result produced by a character repeater to indicate that it has got to the end of a file, and it may be given as input to a character consumer (see below) to indicate that the file is complete and may be closed.

Example of a character repeater in a procedure

The procedure char_file_scr, below, reads characters from a specified file, and prints them on the screen:

```
define char_file_scr(fromfile);
    vars charrep character;
    discin(fromfile) -> charrep;      ;;; Make character repeater.
    repeat
        charrep() -> character;       ;;; Read characters from file
        quitif(character == termin);  ;;; until <TERMIN> is read.
        spr(character);               ;;; Print ASCII code for character.
    endrepeat
enddefine;
```

Each character code returned by the character repeater charrep is assigned to the variable character, and printed (as an integer) on the screen with spaces in between, using spr (see Section 2.8).

To call char_file_scr with the file fromfile (which contains the text for the list [the cat sat on the mat]) as argument, do:

```
char_file_scr('fromfile');
```

This produces the following:

```
91 116 104 101 32 99 97 116 32 115 97 116 32 111 110 32 116 104 101
32 109 97 116 93 10
```

12.3 CHARACTER CONSUMERS

Just as characters may be read from either the terminal or a file, so they can be output to either. Character consumer procedures determine where characters are to be output. They take one input argument, a character code, and produce no result.

12.3.1 charout

The procedure charout is a character consumer which outputs characters to the terminal screen. For example:

```
charout(106);
j

charout(97);
a
```

12.3.2 discout

The user can direct output to a specified file by using the procedure discout.

discout produces a character consumer that outputs characters to a specified file. It takes the name of the file as argument, and produces a character consumer, which the user may assign to a variable. The format is:

```
discout(<filename>) -> consumer;
```

Each time the character consumer held in consumer is called, another character is output to <filename>. To illustrate:

```
discout('tofile') -> charcon;
```

The value of charcon is a character consumer that takes one argument, a character code, and outputs it to the file called tofile. Character codes can either be directly given, or the printed representation of the character code needed can be put in between character quotes. The characters 'k', 'a', 't', 'e' are output to tofile by doing:

```
charcon(`k`); charcon(`a`); charcon(`t`); charcon(`e`);
charcon(termin); ;;; this "closes" the file
```

(A file must be 'opened' if the user wishes to do anything to it. discin and discout open files. When interaction stops, the file must be 'closed', in order subsequently to be readable.)

It would be more convenient if the computer, as opposed to the user, worked out which character code the printed representation of an object stood for. This can be achieved by assigning the character consumer to the variable cucharout, and then using the simple imperative "kate" =>. How this facility works, and what its significance is for the POP-11 printing procedures, is shown below.

12.4 THE DIFFERENCE BETWEEN PR AND CHAROUT

pr arranges for the character codes constituting the printed representation of an object to be sent to whatever output device is indicated by cucharout. The default value of this is charout. Thus the imperative

```
pr(97);
```

causes charout to output the ASCII code for the digit 9 (which is 57) and then the code for the digit 7 (which is 55). Hence the number 97 appears on the screen when the terminal receives these codes.

Unlike pr, charout treats 97 not as an integer to be printed in two digits, but as the single character code 97, which prints as a.

12.4.1 cucharout

All POP-11 printing procedures (for example, pr and =>) use cucharout. Changing the value of cucharout therefore changes the behaviour of the printing procedures. The default value for cucharout is charout, which outputs characters to the terminal screen. By assigning a character consumer to cucharout, the user can determine where output is to be sent. For example, by assigning a consumer produced by discout to the variable cucharout, with

```
discout('tofile') -> cucharout;
```

the user can simply type

```
23 =>
"kate" =>
cucharout(termin);
```

and the file tofile will contain:

```
** 23
** kate
```

The procedure copyfile, below, copies the contents of a file into another file and also onto the terminal screen. It illustrates a situation where it is necessary to assign the character consumer produced by discout to some variable other than cucharout. In this case the value of cucharout must not be altered since output has still to be printed on the terminal screen:

```
define copyfile(fromfile, tofile);
    vars charrep charcon character;
    discout(tofile) -> charcon;  ;;; character consumer CHARCON
    discin(fromfile) -> charrep; ;;; character repeater CHARREP
    until (charrep() ->> character) == termin do
        charcon(character);       ;;; character goes to <tofile>
        cucharout(character);     ;;; character goes to terminal
    enduntil;
    charcon(termin);  ;;; essential to close the output file
enddefine;
```

To call copyfile with the files fromfile and tofile as the input variables, do:

```
copyfile('fromfile', 'tofile');

[the cat sat on the mat]  ;;; this is printed on the terminal screen
```

The file tofile contains: [the cat sat on the mat] .

The user may also assign non I/O procedures to cucharout to alter the effect of pr. The procedure prlength, below, returns the number of characters that would be printed by a call of pr(item). It achieves this by locally redefining cucharout to increment a counter by one for each character that would be output. This could be of use if we wanted to print objects in regular columns, since we would need to know how much space each was going to take up when printed.

```
define prlength(item) -> result;
    define cucharout(character); ;;; locally redefine cucharout
        result + 1 -> result
    enddefine;
    0 -> result;
    pr(item); ;;; counts the number of items that would have been
                ;;; printed without actually printing anything at all.
enddefine;
```

Below are examples showing the new behaviour of pr when called by prlength:

```
prlength("cat") =>
** 3

prlength([1 2 3])=>
** 7
```

Similar techniques may be used to make characters go into a data structure instead of being printed on the terminal.

12.5 CLASS_PRINT

Users may define their own print routines for particular classes of data structure. For example, lists might be represented using round brackets instead of square, and vectors with exclamation marks instead of twiddly brackets. This is achieved by assigning something to the class_print of a data structure. Information about which procedures are used to print data structures is held in the key (see Section 10.3).

The initial value of pr is the procedure syspr. syspr prints the item given to it as argument. If the item is a data structure, syspr does:

```
class_print(datakey(item))(item);
```

datakey takes an item as argument, and returns the key corresponding to the class of the item.

Users can alter the system print routines by changing the class_print procedure. Below is an example of how to print non-embedded lists with round brackets:

```
define pr_lisp_list(list);
    vars x ;
    pr("(");         ;;; print an opening round bracket
    pr(hd(list));
    for x in tl(list)    ;;; print the contents of the rest of the
        pr(space);       ;;; list with spaces in between
        pr(x);
    endfor;
    pr(")")          ;;; print a closing round bracket
enddefine;
```

Calling pr_lisp_list:

```
pr_lisp_list([a b [c d] e]);
(a b [c d] e)
```

The system's print routine for lists is unaltered, as shown below:

```
[a b [c d] e] =>
** [a b [c d] e]
```

By assigning pr_lisp_list to the class print of a list, POP-11's list printing routine is changed. Thus all list brackets in a call of pr_lisp_list([a b [c d] e] ; will be printed out with round brackets, as is done by most LISP systems:

```
pr_lisp_list -> class_print(datakey([any old list]));

[a b [c d] e] =>    ;;; lists are now printed with round brackets
** (a b (c d) e)
```

The normal print routine can be reinstated by doing:

```
sys_syspr -> class_print(datakey([a list]));
```

sys_syspr is the default printing procedure. So after this we get:

```
[a b [c d] e] =>
** [a b [c d] e]
```

12.6 INCHARITEM AND ITEM REPEATERS

An item repeater, like a character repeater, is a procedure that takes no arguments. It produces an item each time it is called. incharitem takes a character repeater as input, and returns an item repeater which the user can assign to a variable. The format is:

```
incharitem(<character repeater>) -> repeater;
```

or

```
incharitem(discin(<filename>)) -> repeater;
```

Each time the item repeater held in repeater is called, another item is returned. When applied to discin(<filename>), incharitem produces an item repeater which reads items from a file. When applied to charin, incharitem produces an item repeater which reads items from the terminal. For example:

```
vars itemrep;
incharitem(charin) -> itemrep; ;;; ITEMREP is an item repeater

itemrep() => ;;; waiting to read and print an item from the terminal
the
** the

itemrep() =>
cat
** cat
```

Examples of an item repeater

The procedure item_to_stop, below, reads items from the terminal up to a full stop. It makes a list of the items read and returns it:

```
define item_to_stop;
    vars itemrep item;
    incharitem(charin) -> itemrep;
    [% until (itemrep() ->> item) = "." do
        item;
        enduntil %]
enddefine;
```

itemrep is the item repeater. Each item it returns is assigned to the variable item, and added to the list. The process continues until the item returned by itemrep is a full stop. We could use item_to_stop in a repeat loop, for example:

```
repeat item_to_stop() => endrepeat;
Sam is a tabby. Tabbies are best.
** [Sam is a tabby]
** [Tabbies are best]
```

The procedure item_file_scr reads items from a file, and prints them on the screen. Note the similarity to char_file_scr, above:

```
define item_file_scr(fromfile);
    vars itemrep item;
    incharitem(discin(fromfile)) -> itemrep;
    until (itemrep() ->> item) = termin do
        spr(item);
    enduntil
enddefine;
```

To call item_file_scr do:

```
item_file_scr('fromfile');
[ the cat sat on the mat ]        ;;; Printed by ITEM_FILE_SCR
```

12.7 ITEM CONSUMERS AND OUTCHARITEM

outcharitem produces an item consumer. It is applied to a character consumer and returns an item consumer, which behaves exactly like pr, except that instead of printing the characters to the terminal via charout, it feeds them to the specified character consumer. Thus, using outcharitem, the user can direct output to a file and the screen in the same procedure since cucharout has not been redefined. For example, the procedure mixoutput outputs items to both the terminal and a file:

```
define mixoutput(file);
    vars outchar outitem list1 list2;
    [this is list1] -> list1;
    [this is list2] -> list2;
    discout(file) -> outchar;     ;;; OUTCHAR = a character consumer
```

```
    outcharitem(outchar) -> outitem; ;;; OUTITEM = an item consumer
    outitem(list1);          ;;; output to the file
    pr('List1 is filed'); ;;; printed on the screen via CHAROUT
    pr(newline);
    outitem(list2);
    pr('List2 is filed');
    pr(newline);
    outitem(newline);
    outitem(termin);          ;;; needed to close the file
enddefine;
```

To call mixoutput, directing some output to the file called mix, do:

```
 mixoutput('mix');
 list1 is filed
 list2 is filed
```

The file mix contains: [this is list1] [this is list2]

12.8 BUFFERING AND RAW MODE

I/O in POP-11 is often buffered. This simply means that the characters are not input or output immediately. They are stored in a data structure like a string, until some condition for 'emptying the buffer' is satisfied, such as the buffer being full, or the user having pressed the <return> key (in the case of charin).

The basic I/O procedures in POP-11 work on devices. These are data structures describing a disc file or some actual device such as a terminal. The devices used by charin and charout are popdevin and popdevout respectively. popdevin is buffered. popdevout is buffered if pop_buffer_charout is true (the default). popdevraw is a 'raw' device, buffered on output only. discin and discout produce buffered device records. Output buffers are 'flushed' automatically when full. The procedure sysflush can be applied to an output device to 'flush' it earlier.

The operating system normally transfers characters to and from the terminal in non-raw mode, but there are occasions when raw mode is more appropriate. In raw mode characters may be read in directly by the program without any intervention by the terminal handler. Also, characters may be output without any transformations, such as printing control characters in a 'readable' form, which some terminal handlers attempt to do. The procedures rawcharin and rawcharout are provided for this purpose. Both use the device popdevraw.

12.8.1 rawcharin
rawcharin is like charin, but uses raw input mode. In this mode, the operating system hands input characters to the user program immediately, for instance without waiting for the user to press <return>. In raw mode the computer neither echoes nor prompts. Every character is a break character, that is, an instruction to the operating system to hand the contents of its input buffer to the user program. For example:

```
 rawcharin() =>  ;;; type a character, say "u", to no prompt. "u" is
                 ;;; not echoed, but returned immediately
 ** 117
```

Example of program using rawcharin

A typical use of rawcharin is in procedures where some key press is purely incidental in initiating some other action. For example, pause, below, suspends the current process until some arbitrary key is pressed. The character produced by this key press is neither prompted nor echoed. The anonymous character is also erased from the stack:

```
define pause;
    pr('press any key to continue...\n');
    erase(rawcharin())  ;;; ignore character put on stack
enddefine;
```

12.8.2 rawcharout

rawcharout is like charout except that it produces 'raw' buffered output. The raw device, popdevraw, is only flushed when one of the following occurs:

   (i) it is full (size 128)
   (ii) sysflush(popdevraw) is called
   (iii) rawcharin( ) is called

popdevout (the buffered device used by charout) is flushed when:

   (i) it is full (size 128)
   (ii) sysflush(popdevout) is called
   (iii) charin( ) is called
   (iv) charout ('\n') is called
   (v) charout(termin) is called

When compiling commands from the terminal, the compiler repeatedly calls charin.

Exercises

1. What is a character repeater? What kind of input does it take? How many arguments does it take? What is its output? Give two examples.
2. How does a character repeater differ from a character consumer? Give two examples of character consumers.
3. What is the default value for the variable cucharout?
4. What would the following imperatives cause to be printed out, and what would be left on the stack?

```
i)   charin() =>
     t

ii)  charin() =>
     Julia

iii) vars itemchar;
     incharitem(charin) -> itemchar;

     itemchar() =>
     t
```

```
iv)  itemchar() =>
     Julia
```

5. Write a procedure called char_file_file that reads characters from one file, and copies them to another file.
6. Define a procedure, showfile, that prints on the screen the entire contents of a file specified by the user.
7. What is a 'break character'?
8. Name two non-raw devices and one raw device.
9. Define a procedure that turns a character consumer into a buffered character consumer, with a 128 character buffer. The procedure should flush the buffer when it is full. Use a list to represent the buffer. Set it off as empty with

```
[] -> buffer;
```

and add the characters to it as they are read in.

Give the procedure, called buffercharout, two input variables, a character, and a character consumer. When the length of the buffer is 128 characters, apply the character consumer to the characters. Use the procedure applist to do this. applist takes two arguments, a list and a procedure, and applies the procedure to each element of the list. Partially apply buffercharout to a character consumer to create a new buffered character consumer.

13

The POP–11 compiler

13.1 COMPILATION

Compilation in POP-11 involves translating the user's input into executable machine code. This is achieved in three stages. First, the input is arranged in a form manipulable by the compiler; second, the input is compiled into virtual machine (VM) code; and third, the VM code is compiled into native machine code and stored in a procedure record which can be executed. How this is achieved is described below.

The POP-11 compiler uses the items held in the list proglist as its input. It works through proglist one item at a time until it becomes empty. Although a pre-constructed list may be used for compilation, it is usually the case that some source of characters, such as the terminal or a disc file, is to be compiled. In this case, proglist is set up by the procedure compile.

compile takes a character repeater, a word, a string or a device record as argument. If its argument is not a character repeater, compile turns it into one. If it is a word or a string, it is taken to be a file name. This is turned into a character repeater by applying discin to it. Similarly, if the argument is a device record, it is turned into a character repeater by applying discin to it. The value of this character repeater is held in the variable cucharin. The stream of characters produced by cucharin is then itemised into a stream of items by the procedure returned by incharitem. Finally, the item repeater produced by incharitem is converted to a dynamic list by pdtolist, and is assigned to the global variable proglist. proglist is effectively a list of all the items in the input stream. It is constructed by:

```
pdtolist(incharitem(cucharin)) -> proglist;
```

The compiler takes items from proglist, one at a time, with the procedure itemread. itemread calls the procedure identprops which returns the syntactic type of an item. Depending on the result, the items are compiled in different ways. Generally, itemread takes items from proglist until a complete expression has been read, that is, an opening and closing syntactic keyword (such as while and endwhile) and the code in between. Syntax words have procedures associated with them (see Syntax Procedures, below). When a closing syntax word is read, its associated procedure calls the appropriate virtual machine code-planting procedures for that sequence. Sequences of VM instructions are stored in the list codelist, which is not directly accessible by the user.

When codelist is complete for a single procedure, the sequences of VM instructions are converted into sequences of machine code instructions by a code generator. The result is stored in a procedure record, and may subsequently be run. This pattern of compilation is shown in Fig. 13.1:

compile sets up proglist

↓

proglist is inspected one item at a time. The
compiler usually removes the items with itemread

↓

key syntax words invoke VM machine code-planting
procedures

↓

codelist: | virtual machine instructions (inaccessible to user) |

_____

↓

code generator translates sequences of VM instructions
into sequences of machine code for complete procedures

↓

procedure record: | Contains real executable machine code |

_____

Figure 13.1 — Compilation.

13.2 MACRO AND SYNTAX WORDS — AN INTRODUCTION

There are two cases where the process of compilation explained above is altered. These are when the identprops of a word taken off proglist are marked "macro" or "syntax". The following sections explain how these items are compiled, and show how users can define their own macro and syntax procedures to extend the POP-11 language.

13.2.1 Macros

Macros can be used to extend the syntax of POP-11. They are also useful for abbreviating commonly used sequences of instructions.

If the identprops of a word is "macro", itemread removes it from the front proglist and looks at its value. A macro can have a procedure, a list, or an item as its value:

(i) If it is a procedure, the procedure is run immediately, and any results replace the macro name at the front of proglist.

(ii) If the value of the macro identifier is a list, the compiler puts all the elements of the list individually onto the front of proglist, rather than just considering the list as a single item.

(iii) If the value of the macro identifier is any other item, then the item replaces the macro name at the front of proglist.

Defining macros

There are two ways to create macros:

```
define macro <macro_name> <input arguments>;
    <body>
enddefine;
```

The input arguments for a macro are set by removing items from proglist, not by taking them from the top of the stack. The same effect can be obtained by declaring the <input arguments> as ordinary local variables of the macro (using vars inside the <body>), and then using itemread to remove items from proglist and assign them to the variables.

```
define macro <macro_name> x y;
    ...
enddefine;
```

is equivalent to:

```
define macro <macro_name>;
    vars x, y;
    itemread() -> x; itemread() -> y;
    ...
enddefine;
```

Macros can also be declared in a vars statement:

```
vars macro <macro_name>;
    <value> -> nonmac <macro_name>;
```

The latter syntax is most appropriate when the value of the macro is to be a list or a single item.

Once used as a macro a word cannot later be used as an ordinary variable without being explicitly reintroduced by a vars statement or being cancelled by doing:

```
cancel <macro_name>; ;;; CANCEL is a macro that simplifies the use
                     ;;; of SYSCANCEL
```

or

```
syscancel("<macro_name>");
```

You can, however, still get at the value of the macro identifier. nonmac preceding <macro_name> stops the expansion of that macro, thus causing it to be treated as an ordinary variable. Similarly, nonop before the name of an infix operator stops the name being treated as infix. nonsyntax does the same job for the syntax procedures described later in this chapter. nonmac, nonop and nonsyntax are generally used when you want to use the value of the identifier as the input to a procedure call, as in:

```
pr(nonop +);          ;;; Show me the current value of "+"
<procedure +>

vars plus_times ; nonop + <> nonop * -> plus_times;
plus_times(3,4,5) =>  ;;; PLUS_TIMES is a procedure which adds its
** 27                 ;;; second two arguments and multiplies them
                      ;;; by its first (a bit confusing, perhaps,
                      ;;; but it does illustrate the use of NONOP)
```

Examples of macro identifiers whose values are procedures

The procedure sysdaytime returns the current date and time as a string:

```
sysdaytime () =>
** Fri Dec 14 14:58:19 GMT 1984
```

To abbreviate sysdaytime( ) =>, we can make it the body of a macro identifier, say t for 'time':

```
define macro t;
    "sysdaytime", ;;; put the word "sysdaytime" on the stack
    "(",          ;;; put the word "(" on the stack
    ")",          ;;; put the word ")" on the stack
    "=>"          ;;; put the word "=>" on the stack
enddefine;
```

identprops shows t to be marked as a macro:

```
identprops("t") =>
** macro
```

Whenever t appears at the front of proglist, the compiler replaces the macro name with the results of running the procedure. Thus the words "sysdaytime", "(", ")", and "=>" are put on the front of proglist ready to be compiled. For example:

```
define double(x);
    x * 2 =>
    t    ;;; macro abbreviation for "sysdaytime() =>"
enddefine;

double(2); ;;; calling DOUBLE with 2 as argument
** 4
** Fri Dec 14 15:36:19 GMT 1984
```

The macro was expanded when it was read. This was inside the definition of double, so the words "sysdaytime", "(", ")" and "=>" were read as part of the definition of double. double therefore contains a call of sysdaytime.

We might have wanted t to print out the date and time as soon as we typed it, rather than planting a call of sysdaytime inside double. To achieve this, we could have defined the macro as:

```
define macro t;
    sysdaytime() =>
enddefine;
```

Here the macro does not produce results to be added to the front of proglist. Rather, it prints out the date and time as soon as it is called, that is, as soon as itemread removes it from proglist. So if we had typed t while we were in the middle of defining double, the effect of running the macro procedure would have been to get the date and time printed immediately. proglist is unaltered since the macro t now leaves no result on the stack. double does not now contain a call of sysdaytime:

```
define double(x);
   x * 2 =>
   t            ;;; macro T run there and then
** Fri Dec 14 15:43:01 GMT 1984  ;;; result of T printed immediately
enddefine;
```

swap, below, is an example of a macro with arguments. It swaps the values of two variables:

```
define macro swap x y;
    x, ",", y, "->", x, "->", y, ";";
enddefine;
```

This could have been written as:

```
define macro swap;
    vars x y;
    itemread() -> x; ;;; assign the next item on PROGLIST to X
    itemread() -> y; ;;; assign the following item on PROGLIST to Y
    x, ",", y, "->", x, "->", y, ";";
enddefine;
```

The macro identifier swap is replaced by x, y —> x —> y; at the front of proglist. This is then read from proglist by compile, which plants machine code to swap the values of x and y.

```
vars var1, var2;
3 -> var1; 4 -> var2;
swap var1 var2      ;;; run the macro SWAP. X,Y -> X -> Y; is put on
                    ;;; the front of PROGLIST, and then compiled
                    ;;; and executed.

var1 =>             ;;; variable values are now swapped
** 4
var2 =>
** 3
```

Examples of macros with non-procedural values

The following macro defines a new print arrow, written as _>. Following an expression with _> causes the dataword of the object which is the expression's value to be printed out before the object.

myprint, below, is the procedure that will be run at compile time when the macro identifier _> is read:

```
define myprint(x);
    pr(newline); spr("**");
    spr("the");
    spr(dataword(x));
    pr(x)
enddefine;

myprint(23);      ;;; calling MYPRINT with 23 as argument

** the integer 23
```

The macro _> can be defined as:

```
vars macro _>; [; myprint(); ] -> nonmac _>;
```

Whenever _> is read, the items in the list brackets replace it at the front of proglist, for example:

```
23 _>                ;;; at compile time the _> expands to ; myprint();
** the integer 23    ;;; 23 becomes the input variable for MYPRINT

[a b c] _>           ;;; calling _>
** the pair [a b c]  ;;; the result of _>
```

The value of the macro is a list, which is added to the front of proglist. This list is the same every time you use the macro — it produces different effects because there are different things on the stack each time you use it.

We can define another macro, debug, which provides a useful debugging aid. debug will also have a list rather than a procedure as its value:

```
vars macro debug;
[; if debugging then database ==> endif;] -> nonmac debug;
```

Each time debug is read, a conditional statement will be inserted into the program. This statement has the effect that, when the program is running, if the variable debugging has a non-<false> value, then the database will be printed out. If you insert the word debug at various points in your program, you can get it to print out information about the current state of the database as it proceeds by setting debugging to <true>, or you can get it to run normally by setting debugging to <false>.

Suppose we have a word declared as a macro name with a single item as its associated value. When the compiler removes the macro identifier from the front of proglist, it replaces it with the item which is its value. For example:

```
vars macro leap_year; 366 -> nonmac leap_year;
```

Every time the word leap_year is found at the front of proglist, it will be replaced by 366. This is different from

```
vars leap_year; 366 -> leap_year;
```

where the value of the variable leap_year is retrieved every time it is read, and there would be nothing to stop the value of leap_year changing. Using macros for things like leap_year is fairly similar to declaring them as constants. The code that is generated for cases like this is marginally more efficient if you use a macro than if you use a constant, but it takes longer to compile.

13.2.2 Syntax procedures

Users may define new syntax words to extend the language. For example, if the various looping constructs such as until, repeat, and while did not already exist, they could be added by defining new syntax procedures.

Syntax procedures take no arguments and produce no results. They simply plant virtual machine instructions in codelist. They are written in POP-11, and are the lowest level at which the user may program. Syntax procedures take the following format:

```
define syntax <syntax_name>;
    <body>
enddefine;
```

Closing syntax words must be declared in vars statements:

```
vars syntax <syntax_name>
```

Syntax procedures are run at compile time. When itemread reads the syntax identifier name, the VM instructions are planted in codelist straight away. Items do not have to be added to the front of proglist and then compiled. Syntax procedures are therefore more efficient than macros. They also provide more informative mishap messages if illegal syntax is used. With macros comprehensive syntactic error checking will only happen if explicitly encoded in the macro by the user.

Examples of syntax procedures

loop . . . endloop, below, illustrates how to define new syntax words. Its behaviour simulates the repeat forever . . . endrepeat loop.

```
vars syntax endloop;   ;;; closing syntax words must be declared as
                       ;;; syntax words with the VARS syntax

define syntax loop;
    vars lab;
    sysNEW_LABEL() -> lab;    ;;; generate a label
    sysLABEL(lab);            ;;; plant it
```

```
    systxsqcomp("endloop") ->;  ;;; compile until the next "endloop"
    sysGOTO(lab);               ;;; plant jump back to start
enddefine;

identprops("loop") =>
** syntax

identprops("endloop") =>
** syntax
```

Call loop:

```
loop "hello" => endloop; ;;; this will go on forever unless the user
** hello                 ;;; interrupts it
** hello
** hello
```

When the compiler reads the syntax word loop, it generates and plants a label. The procedure systxsqcomp (Terminated eXpression SeQuence COMPile) is called. This compiles and plants code for a sequence of expressions separated by commas or semicolons up to the closing syntax word. In this case "hello" => is compiled. The word endloop marks the end of the expression and is returned and ignored. The label is accessed again and the process is repeated indefinitely until it is interrupted by the user. (We use the assignment arrow immediately followed by a semicolon to throw away a result that we are not interested in, as described in Section 3.6.)

Using the closing syntax word endrepeat instead of endloop causes a mishap message because the compiler is searching for the syntax word endloop:

```
loop "hello" => endrepeat;  ;;; MISHAP because searching for closing
                            ;;; syntax word ENDLOOP:

;;; MISHAP - MSW: MISPLACED SYNTAX WORD
;;; INVOLVING: FOUND endrepeat READING TO endloop
;;; DOING    : loop compile
```

Our second example will allow you to write programs in which assignment goes from right to left. The format will be:

```
let <var> be <expression>
```

Below we declare be as a syntax word, and define let:

```
constant syntax be;

define syntax let();
    vars target;
    set_assign:
    itemread() -> target;       ;;; Read the variable to be assigned
    unless  itemread() == "be"  ;;; Check next word is BE
    then    mishap('BE not read when expected', nil)
    endunless;
    sysxcomp();                 ;;; Compile the expression denoting
                                ;;; the new value.
```

```
     sysPOP(target);           ;;; Plant code to assign it
     if      systry(",")       ;;; If the expression ended with a
     then    goto set_assign   ;;; comma, there are more
     endif;                    ;;; assignments to be done
enddefine;
```

```
let x be 1 + 2; x =>
** 3
let x be [1 2 3 4], y be 46; x => y =>
** [1 2 3 4]
** 46
```

Both our examples made use of numerous system procedures which we have barely explained at all. Our hope is that the examples give you a feel for the sorts of extensions that may be made, rather than enabling you to make such extensions for yourself. If you want to define your own syntax procedures, and the POP-11 you are using is part of a POPLOG system, then you can look in the file ref syscompile for descriptions of all the building blocks you will need for planting code. We will say no more about these procedures here.

13.3 SUMMARY OF DIFFERENT TYPES OF PROCEDURE NAMES

Procedures come in four types: normal, infix, macro and syntax. Strictly speaking, it is names of procedures that come in four types — their values are in all cases simply procedure records. The differences are concerned with what happens when programs using the names are being compiled. Macros are run at read time, and syntax procedures are run at compile time, as explained above. The remaining two are 'normal' procedures and 'infix' operators. We have seen what these procedures do before — in Chapters 3 and 4 — but it is worth summarising it again here to clarify the differences between them and syntax and macro procedures.

Normal procedures

A normal procedure is one which is invoked by writing its name, followed by an opening parenthesis, its arguments (if any) separated by commas and finally a closing parenthesis, for example:

```
proc(x + 1, y)
```

This compiles into instructions to apply the procedure which is the current value of the variable proc to the results of evaluating the expressions x + 1 and y.

Infix operators

An infix operator is invoked by placing the name between its arguments. Infix operators usually have two arguments. For example + is an infix operator, as in:

```
3 + 4;
```

It is not essential for such a procedure to have two arguments. An infix operator of one argument must be placed before its argument, for example $- x -> y$; a name of this kind is called a 'prefix' operator.

Infix operators have a numerical precedence to disambiguate expressions such as:

```
3 + 4 * 5
```

13.4 THE POP—11 ERROR HANDLER

We have seen numerous examples of procedures containing calls of mishap, and of the results of such calls. mishap produces error messages to tell you what went wrong when your program was running. We can get more information than merely an error message and a list of items that were involved in the error condition by using the procedure popready, defined below. Before we discuss popready itself, we will look at what mishap does. mishap could have been defined as:

```
define mishap ();
    prmishap();
    interrupt();
    setpop();
enddefine;
```

It is a procedure which simply calls three other procedures in turn. prmishap prints out the error messages that were passed into mishap. Note that mishap does not have any explicit arguments, so that anything which is on the stack when it is called is passed straight on to prmishap. The standard value of prmishap is something like:

```
define prmishap(message, culprits);
    spr(';;; MISHAP ' >< message); print(newline);
    spr(';;; INVOLVING: ' >< culprits); print(newline);
    spr(';;; DOING ');
    print_calling_sequence();
enddefine;
```

This is not a complete definition of prmishap, since it contains a call of an undefined procedure, print_calling_sequence, which would be quite hard to define with the facilities we have seen so far. (It could be defined using some of the more advanced notions in Chapter 14.) It is, nevertheless, a reasonable sketch of what prmishap should do.

The user may redefine prmishap to do different things. One quite common way of redefining it is so that it traps some specified error condition for which you have a solution, as in:

```
define prmishap (message, culprits);
    if      message = 'DIVIDING BY 0 OR ARITHMETIC OVERFLOW'
    then    10000000; exitfrom(mishap);
    else    sysprmishap(message, culprits)
    endif;
enddefine;
```

This alters prmishap so that if the error that was detected was an attempt to do some arithmetic operation which led to the creation of an over-large number, the operation succeeds and the result is assumed to be 10000000. Note that the redefinition of prmishap calls exitfrom, which shall be described in Section 14.2. If it was any other error condition, it should be dealt with normally, so just pass the arguments on to sysprmishap, which is the default value of prmishap.

After prmishap has been called to provide a description of what went wrong, interrupt is called to tidy things up. interrupt is also user definable. Its default value is setpop. setpop clears away anything you have typed which has not yet been read by the system, unwinds all the procedure calls which have not yet returned, and resets the system so that it is waiting for you to type something for it to compile and execute. Once setpop has been called, there is no way for you to inspect the details of the situation in which the error handler was invoked, since they will all have been tidied away. It is sometimes useful to be able to inspect the values of local variables when the error handler is invoked. Assigning popready to be the value of interrupt makes this possible. popready is defined something like:

```
define popready ();
    pr('POPREADY\n');
    compile(charin);
    pr('Leaving POPREADY\n');
enddefine;
```

popready contains a call of compile, so that anything you type after popready has been entered will be compiled and executed. If you assign popready to be the value of interrupt, it will get called in exactly the situation where the error handler was invoked. All values of local variables, etc., will be exactly as they were when the error was discovered, so you can inspect them by simply typing their names followed by the print arrow. The call of compile will access the variable values which are current at the time when it is invoked, which will be the ones they had when the error occurred. compile will go on reading and executing commands until it reaches the end of the input stream, usually indicated by typing <ctrl>&Z or <ctrl>&D, at which point it will exit. popready will then print out its second message, and return to mishap, which will now call setpop to tidy things up as usual.

The built-in definition of popready is a bit more complicated than the definition given above, but it is essentially the same. The use of popready within the error handler can make it much easier to debug your programs. You may also find that including explicit calls of popready in your programs when you are debugging them can help you keep track of what is happening.

Exercises
1. How is proglist constructed?
2. When are sequences of VM code compiled into machine code?
3. What are the main differences between syntax and macro procedures?

4. Write a macro to abbreviate 'vars item; for item in list do' called fild. Write a macro called efild to correspond to endfor. It should then be possible to write the following procedure:

```
define len(list) —> total;
    0 —> total;
    fild
        1 + total —> total
    efild
enddefine;
```

14

Non-standard
control structures

'Control structure' is the name for the organisation under which operations are performed when running a program, and for the sequence those operations are run in. We might, for example, refer to control as being in a loop, being recursive, passing from one procedure to another, or not returning to a procedure.

POP-11 provides a number of non-standard control structures, which can be used to construct elegant, efficient solutions to problems which would otherwise be awkward to solve.

This chapter makes the standard control structure explicit, illustrating it with some simple procedures. Then non-standard control structures are introduced, using modifications of these same basic procedures for examples. This will show us how the procedures chain, exitfrom, exitto, chainfrom, chainto and catch and throw effect extremely non-standard control structures. Continuing the theme, POP-11 processes are introduced. Processes provide a way of encapsulating a state of the POP-11 world, to be returned to at strategic times. Finally, continuation programming in POP-11 is explained.

14.1 STANDARD CONTROL STRUCTURE

We start with three extremely simple procedures, a, b, and c, which just print out messages stating what they are doing and how far they have got, and do some simple arithmetic as they go. a calls b, which calls c:

```
define c;
    pr('running C'); pr(newline);
    x * 2 -> x; x =>
    pr('C finished'); pr(newline);
enddefine;
```

```
define b;
    vars x;
    pr('running B'); pr(newline);
    x * 2 -> x; x =>
    c();
    pr('continuing to run B'); pr(newline);
    x =>
    pr('B finished'); pr(newline);
enddefine;

define a;
    vars x;
    pr('running A'); pr(newline);
    3 -> x; x =>
    b();
    pr('continuing to run A'); pr(newline);
    x =>
    pr('A finished'); pr(newline);
enddefine;
```

The standard flow of control is as follows: procedure a runs until the call of procedure b. Control passes to procedure b. The point in a at which this happens is stored on the 'calling stack'. b passes control to c in the same way, and c is run until it finishes. Control then passes back to the point in b at which it was suspended (this point having been stored on the calling stack, as described above). Now b finishes. Control passes to the remaining instructions in procedure a. Finally a finishes. This sequence of events can be illustrated by the following diagram:

a calls b
   b calls c
      c runs and finishes
   Control passes to remaining instructions in b. b finishes.
Control passes to remaining instructions in a. a finishes.

The chain of procedures which is created is known as the calling sequence. All the information needed for keeping track of what is going on is kept in an area called the calling stack, (sometimes called the auxiliary stack). This stack is used for saving the point each procedure had got to when it transferred control to something which it was calling, and for looking after the values of local variables. By calling procedure a, we can follow the flow of control, and also see how the value of the variable x changes as we go up and down the calling stack (see Section 2.10 for the difference between local and global variables):

```
a();
```

```
running A
** 3           ;;; X is 3 in A and is local.
running B
** 6           ;;; X is 6 in B and is local. (The value X had in A is
running C       ;;; still valid when it is accessed in B.)
** 12          ;;; X is 12 in C and is global. X will not be reset
```

```
C finished      ;;; when control passes back to B from C.
continuing to run B
** 12           ;;; X is 12 in B - it wasn't reset when C finished
                ;;; since it is not local to C.
B finished
continuing to run A
** 3            ;;; X is 3 in A - reset when B exited because
                ;;; it is local to B.
A finished
```

14.2 LOW LEVEL PROCEDURES FOR NON-STANDARD CONTROL

By using procedures for non-standard control, the user can alter the behaviour of the above procedures. For example, procedures in the calling stack may be by-passed, and local variable values may fail to be reset. The following procedures provide the basic facilities required for implementation of non-standard control structures.

chain

The procedure chain takes one argument, a procedure. When a procedure, p, calls chain, control is immediately transferred to chain's argument. Any remaining instructions in p are never executed. Local variable values are not passed on from p to the procedure called by chain. When the procedure given as argument to chain is run, all variable values are set to what they were when p inherited them. When the procedure chained to finishes, control returns to the procedure which originally called p.

Example

Procedure b, below, has been altered to call chain(c) rather than calling c normally:

```
define b;
    vars x;
    pr('running B'); pr(newline);
    x * 2 -> x; x =>
    chain(c);  ;;; the call to CHAIN to procedure C
    x =>
    pr('B finished'); pr(newline);
enddefine;
```

The effect of the different control structure can be seen when we run a:

```
a();
running A
** 3       ;;; X is 3 in A
running B
** 6       ;;; X is 6 in B. This value for X will not be passed on
           ;;; to C, as it is local to B. At this point C is
           ;;; CHAINed to.
running C  ;;; X is reset to what it was before entry to B, i.e. 3.
** 6       ;;; C immediately doubles X's value and prints it out.
```

```
C finished
continuing to run A
** 6         ;;; X is global to C, and is therefore not reset when
             ;;; control returns from C to A (not to B)
A finished
```

The caller of chain, procedure b, is exited from, and a chain to c is made. The value of x in c is set as it was when b inherited it, that is, to what it was in a. When c finishes, control returns to a, not, as would normally be the case, to b. The instructions in b after the call of c are never executed. Since x is not local to c, its value is not reset in a.

chain is the most basic procedure for implementing non-standard control strategies. Several of the procedures introduced below could be defined simply using chain.

exitfrom

The procedure exitfrom takes one argument, a procedure higher up in the calling stack than the caller. Control leaves the caller immediately exitfrom is called. Instructions in the caller and the called procedure, and instructions in procedures in the calling stack in between the two, are never finished. All values of variables which are local to procedures in between the caller of exitfrom and the procedure control returns to are reset appropriately.

Example

Procedure c, below, has been altered to call exitfrom (b) (a and b are the same as in the standard control structure example.)

```
define c;
    pr('running C'); pr(newline);
    x * 2 -> x; x =>
    exitfrom(b);  ;;; the call of EXITFROM(B)
    pr('C finished'); pr(newline);
enddefine;
```

The effect of the different control structure can be seen when we run a:

```
a();
running A
** 3       ;;; X is 3 in A
running B
** 6       ;;; X is 6 in B
running C
** 12      ;;; X is 12 in C
continuing to run A  ;;; Got here by going to the point in B where
                     ;;; C was called and immediately exiting
                     ;;; from B. X, which is local to B, is reset
** 3                 ;;; to 3
A finished
```

Procedures c and b are never completed. When control unwinds up the calling stack to the end of b, the value of x is reset to 3 — its value in a.

exitto

The procedure exitto takes one argument, a procedure higher up in the calling stack than the caller. Control leaves the caller immediately exitto is called. Any remaining instructions in the caller, and those procedures between it and the target on the calling stack, are never executed. Local variable values are reset as control unwinds up the calling stack to the target procedure. The target procedure, and procedures above it in the calling stack, are continued normally.

The difference between exitto and exitfrom is that exitto returns control to the procedure given as exitto's argument, whereas exitfrom returns control to the procedure which called exitfrom's argument.

Example
Procedure c, below, has been altered to call exitto(a) (a and b are the same as in the standard control structure example):

```
define c;
    pr('running C'); pr(newline);
    x * 2 -> x; x =>
    exitto(a);
    pr('C finished'); pr(newline);
enddefine;
```

Again the effect of the different control structure can be seen when we run a:

```
a();
running A
** 3
running B
** 6
running C
** 12     ;;; EXITTO command executed here
continuing to run A    ;;; value of X reset
** 3
A finished    ;;; only procedure A is finished
```

Procedure c is exited from immediately. Control goes straight back to a. The local variables in procedure a are reset. a is then finished off. This has the same effect as doing exitfrom(b), as above.

When to use exitto and exitfrom
Use exitfrom(x) if you want control to pass to the procedure which calls x.
Use exitto(x) if you know exactly where you want to go to.

chainfrom

The procedure chainfrom takes two arguments. Both are procedures. The calling stack is unwound to the first argument. From there a chain is made to the second argument. When the second argument has been run, control unwinds up the calling stack, as normal. For this example, a new procedure, d, is defined below. c is also redefined, but a and b stay as they were in the standard control structure example:

```
define d;
    vars x;   ;;; X is local to D
    pr('running D'); pr(newline);
    x * 2 -> x; x =>
    pr('D finished'); pr(newline);
enddefine;
```

```
define c;
    pr('running C'); pr(newline);
    x * 2 -> x; x =>
    chainfrom(b,d);
    pr('C finished'); pr(newline);
enddefine;
```

When chainfrom(b, d) is executed in c, control unwinds up the calling stack to b. From there a chain to d is made and d is run. Control then continues up the calling stack. It begins where it would have gone after exiting from b had the chainfrom not happened:

```
a();
running A    ;;; X is 3 in A
** 3
running B    ;;; X is 6 in B
** 6
running C    ;;; Local variable values not passed on since X is
** 12        ;;; global. Control unwinds to B and then CHAINs
             ;;; to D. X, which is local to B, is reset.
running D
** 6         ;;; D made X 6
D finished
continuing to run A   ;;; continues back up the calling stack
** 3
A finished
```

chainto

The procedure chainto takes two arguments. Unlike chainfrom, a chain does not actually take place. Control unwinds from the caller to the target (the first argument). The procedure in the second argument is then simply run. When it finishes, control returns to the target and continues up the calling stack. c is redefined for this example. a, b and d remain as they were for the chainfrom example:

```
define c;
    pr('running C'); pr(newline);
    x * 2 -> x;
    x =>
    chainto(a,d);
    pr('C finished'); pr(newline);
enddefine;
```

```
a();
running A
** 3          ;;; X is 3 in A
running B
** 6          ;;; X is 6 in B
running C
** 12         ;;; X is 12 in C. At this point, control unwinds to A.
              ;;; X gets reset to 3 as it unwinds past B.
running D     ;;; D is run from within A.
** 6          ;;; X is 6 in D
D finished    ;;; X is local to D, thus value reset to 3 when D finishes
continuing to run A
** 3
A finished
```

caller

In addition to providing facilities for by-passing the normal calling stack (like exitfrom, chain and so on), POP-11 also allows programs to examine the calling stack using the procedure caller. caller takes one argument, an integer (N), and returns the procedure which is in the calling stack N levels above the call of caller. Thus, caller(0) means the procedure that called caller, caller(1) means the caller of that procedure, and so on. The object returned by caller is simply the procedure record of the procedure in question. We define the procedure test, below, to print out its caller(0):

```
define test;
    caller(0) =>
enddefine;
```

To call test do:

```
test( );
** <procedure test>
```

Using caller and chain we can re-implement exitto, exitfrom, chainto and chainfrom. myexitto, below, shows how exitto could be implemented:

```
define myexitto(p);
    unless caller(1) = p then
        chain(p, myexitto, chain); ;;; MYEXITTO left on the stack to
    endunless ;                    ;;; be picked up by CHAIN, p to
enddefine;                         ;;; be picked up by MYEXITTO.
```

14.3 CATCH AND THROW

The above procedures provide great flexibility, but can be awkward to use coherently. They are normally used as the basis of more structured mechanisms. catch and throw are standard procedures which provide a structured version of the same ideas. The illustration of how to use catch and throw is more practical than the ones we used to make all the intricacies of the low level procedures clear.

catch takes three arguments. Its format is:

```
catch(<procedure>, <catch_procedure>, <spec>)
```

The first argument, <procedure>, is a procedure, which is called immediately. If, while this procedure is running, the procedure throw is called with an argument that matches <spec>, and if <catch_procedure> is a procedure, control unwinds to this call of catch and <catch_procedure> is run. The matching is done using matches. (If <catch_procedure> is not a procedure, it is simply left on the stack.) After this, control returns from the call of catch. If throw's argument does not match <spec>, control unwinds until a call of catch whose <spec> does match is found. This makes it possible to embed procedures which use catch and throw inside one another, and yet for each instance of throw to be able to specify which instance of catch it is aiming at.

The procedure test, below, illustrates how, using the control structures created by catch and throw, we can walk recursively through a tree of numbers looking for ones that do not fall within certain bounds. As soon as we find one, we exit from test with a description of what we found and what was wrong with it, without having to worry about how far through our recursive search of the tree we were when we found the offending item.

test takes three arguments — a list of lists of numbers, a number specifying a lower bound, and a number specifying an upper bound. It immediately calls catch. The procedure given to catch as argument, checklist, is run. checklist recursively checks to see if any of the numbers in the tree fall outside the bounds specified. If a number is outside the bounds then throw is called. The argument given to throw in both cases matches the third argument of catch, namely [nogood ?culprit ?reason], so control unwinds to catch, and the second argument of catch, the procedure catcher, is run.

```
define checklist(tree, Lo, Hi);
    vars x ;
    ;;; recursively check if elements of tree are in bounds
    if      islist(tree)    ;;; if the argument is actually a tree
    then    for x in tree   ;;; then check each component (which
            do  checklist(x, Lo, Hi) ;;; may itself be a tree)
            endfor;
    elseif  tree > Hi       ;;; otherwise see if it's too big
    then    throw([nogood ^tree toobig]) ;;; unwind to catch if so
    elseif  tree < Lo       ;;; see if it's too small
    then    throw([nogood ^tree toolow]) ;;; unwind to catch
    else tree =>            ;;; OK - print out to see where we are
    endif
enddefine;


define test(tree, Lo, Hi);
    vars culprit reason;
    define catcher();  ;;; CATCHER is locally defined
```

```
        ;;; This will be run if a number is out of bounds
        [rejected ^culprit because ^reason] =>
    enddefine;
    ;;; recursively examine the tree and complain if necessary
    tree, Lo, Hi;    ;;; Arguments for checklist put on stack
    catch(checklist, catcher, [nogood ?culprit ?reason])
enddefine;
```

Below are examples of test being run:

```
trace checklist test throw ;

test([1 2 [2.5] 3], 0, 6);     ;;; Try TEST on a case where all elements
> test [1 2 [2.5] 3] 0 6       ;;; are in bounds
!> checklist [1 2 [2.5] 3] 0 6
!!> checklist 1 0 6
** 1                           ;;; When checklist gets a number which
                               ;;; is OK it prints it out
!!< checklist
!!> checklist 2 0 6
** 2
!!< checklist
!!> checklist [2.5] 0 6
!!!> checklist 2.5 0 6
** 2.5
!!!< checklist
!!< checklist
!!> checklist 3 0 6
** 3
!!< checklist
!< checklist
< test
```

```
vars tree ;
[3 [3.3 3.4 [3.45 2.6 [9]] [2 4.6]]] -> tree;
test(tree, 1, 3.4);            ;;; An example with some items too big
> test [3 [3.3 3.4 [3.45 2.6 [9]] [2 4.6]]] 1 3.4
!> checklist [3 [3.3 3.4 [3.45 2.6 [9]] [2 4.6]]] 1 3.4
!!> checklist 3 1 3.4
** 3                           ;;; First number tested is OK
!!< checklist
!!> checklist [3.3 3.4 [3.45 2.6 [9]] [2 4.6]] 1 3.4
!!!> checklist 3.3 1 3.4
** 3.3                         ;;; So is second
!!!< checklist
!!!> checklist 3.4 1 3.4
** 3.4                         ;;; and third
!!!< checklist
!!!> checklist [3.45 2.6 [9]] 1 3.4
!!!!> checklist 3.45 1 3.4     ;;; But this one's too big
!!!!!!> throw [nogood 3.45 toobig] ;;; So we THROW it
** [rejected 3.45 because toobig] ;;; The catcher reports its catch
< test                         ;;; and TEST immediately exits
```

The use of catch and throw has enabled us to define checklist so that it reacts immediately it finds something it does not like. We have not had to worry about how control returns from checklist when this happens — the call of throw looks after it for us.

14.4 PROCESSES

A state of the POP-11 world can be encapsulated in a process record. Doing this allows the user to swap the process in and out of the control structure. For example, processes can be run, suspended (whereupon something else takes over), resumed and killed. The important parts of the POP-11 world that are stored in the process are the contents of the calling stack, and the contents of the user stack. Specifically, a procedure, or part of a procedure, can be made into a process. A process in POP-11 is a data structure containing the following information:

(i) the state of the calling stack.

(ii) the values of local variables of procedures in the calling stack.

(iii) the state of the user stack at the time that the procedure would be run, so that values can be passed from the ordinary user stack to the process' version of it — processes have their own stacks.

There are two procedures available for making processes, consprocto and consproc.

consprocto

The procedure consprocto returns a process constructed from part of the current calling stack. It takes two arguments. Its format is:

```
consprocto(<n>, <procedure>)
```

The first argument, $<n>$, is an integer. $<n>$ items are passed from the user stack to the process' stack. The items are removed from the user stack when the process is created. The second argument, $<procedure>$, is a procedure. It must be in the current calling sequence above the call of consprocto. The process saves the state of execution from where it is called, up to and including the procedure $<procedure>$. When the process is called, execution continues from the point it was at when the process was created. As control unwinds back up the calling stack, only those procedures which were in the part of the stack which was saved at that time will be continued. On exit from $<procedure>$ the process terminates, no matter what the original situation when $<procedure>$ was called was like.

A process created by consprocto captures the state of the system at the time the process was created.

consproc

The procedure consproc returns a process constructed from a procedure. It takes two arguments. Its format is:

```
consproc(<n>, <procedure>)
```

<n> is the same as for consprocto, above. <procedure> is a procedure. The process is made from this procedure. When the process is run for the first time the procedure is called in the normal way. When the procedure exits, the process terminates.

runproc

The procedure runproc runs a given process. It takes two arguments. Its format is:

```
runproc(<n>, <process>)
```

<n> is an integer. <n> items are passed from the user stack to the process' stack. <process> is a process.

suspend

The procedure suspend passes control back to a caller of the current process. The state of execution at the point when suspend is called is stored in the original process record. Control returns from the call of runproc which ran the target process. The suspended process may later be restarted.

suspend takes one or two arguments. Its formats are:

```
suspend(<n>)
```

and

```
suspend(<n>, <to_process>)
```

<n> is an integer. <n> items are passed as results from the process stack to the user stack. The second argument is a process. All processes up to and including <to_process> are suspended. If this argument is omitted, only the current process is suspended.

ksuspend

The procedure ksuspend takes the same arguments as suspend. Its formats are:

```
ksuspend(<n>)
```

and

```
ksuspend(<n>, <to_process>)
```

<n> is the same as for suspend, above. All processes up to and including <to_process> are killed. If <to_process> is omitted only the current process is killed. <n> items are passed to the user stack, and control returns to the call of runproc.

Recursive calls of runproc

If runproc is called recursively, the first process suspends itself while control transfers to the second process. When the second process finishes or suspends, control returns to the process which called it.

resume
The procedure resume passes control from one process to another. Its format is:

```
resume(<n>, <resume_process>)
```

or

```
resume(<n>, <suspend_process>, <resume_process>)
```

The current process, or several processes if <suspend_process> is included, is suspended, and control passes to the process in <resume_process>. <n> represents how many items to pass from the original process' stack to the invoked process' stack.

kresume
The procedure kresume is like resume, except that it kills the current process, or all processes up to and including <kill_process>. Its formats are:

```
kresume(<n>, <resume_process>)
```

and

```
kresume(<n>, <kill_process>, <resume_process>)
```

isliveprocess
As with most data types, POP-11 provides a recogniser, isprocess, which returns <true> if given a process and <false> if given anything else. For processes it is also often useful to know whether the process has terminated or not. You might, for instance, be simulating a parallel system by embodying each component as a process and running them in strict rotation. You would not want to try running a process which had terminated, even if it was its turn, since this would be treated as an error. isliveprocess tells you whether a process can be resumed (or run) or not.

Exercises
1. Make a process which will be killed after being run once and have no specified place to return control to. Make it return the same integer given it as argument.

    What will happen if you try to run the process for a second time?
2. What will be the result of the imperative runproc(0, process1) given the two processes below:

```
vars procedure1 procedure2 process1 process2;
```

```
define procedure1;
    vars x;
    for x from 1 to 5 do
        pr(x); pr(","); runproc(0, process2)
    endfor
enddefine;

define procedure2;
    vars x;
    for x from 1 to 5 do
        pr(x); pr(newline); ksuspend(0)
    endfor
enddefine;

consproc(0, procedure1) -> process1;
consproc(0, procedure2) -> process2;
```

Example

We will illustrate the use of processes by considering the 'same fringe' problem, where we want to see if the 'fringes' of two trees are the same.

Comparing the fringes of two trees

The 'fringe' of a tree is the sequence of items you would obtain if you were to enumerate its terminal nodes working from left to right. For instance, the fringes of the trees

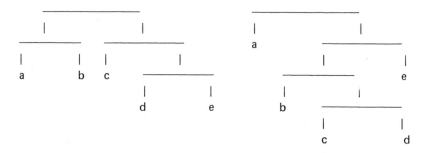

are both [a b c d e]. The program we want to write is one which will compare the fringes of two trees. The problem with this task is that if we use the natural recursive algorithm for enumerating the terminal nodes of the two trees, we will have great difficulty keeping the two enumerations in step. The fact that the two trees to be compared will in general be different shapes means that the recursion will operate differently on each of them.

We can use the following procedure to enumerate the fringe of a given tree (where a tree is being represented as a nested list).

```
define fringe(tree);
    vars x;
    if      islist(tree)    ;;; if we've really got a tree we want
```

```
        then    for x in tree   ;;; to look at each subtree in turn
                do  fringe(x)    ;;; and enumerate its fringe
                endfor
        else    tree =>          ;;; if we have a terminal, display it
        endif;
    enddefine;
```

To see this in action try it on our first tree:

```
    trace fringe;

    fringe([[a b] [c [d e]]]);    ;;; get the fringe of our first tree
    > fringe [[a b] [c [d e]]]
    !> fringe [a b]
    !!> fringe a
    ** a                          ;;; first element of fringe
    !!< fringe
    !!> fringe b
    ** b                          ;;; second
    !!< fringe
    !< fringe
    !> fringe [c [d e]]
    !!> fringe c
    ** c
        ...                       ;;; tracing edited out
    ** d
        ...
    ** e
```

We could alter fringe so it just piled up the elements on the stack, and then
using decorated list brackets we could collect these elements into a list.

```
    define fringe(tree);
        vars x;
        if      islist(tree)    ;;; if we've really got a tree we want
        then    for x in tree   ;;; to look at each subtree in turn
                do  fringe(x)    ;;; and enumerate its fringe
                endfor
        else    tree            ;;; if we have a terminal, stack it
        endif;
    enddefine;


    define listfringe(tree);
        [% fringe(tree) %]      ;;; collect the fringe in a list
    enddefine;
```

Using listfringe we could compare the fringes of two trees by collecting them in
two lists and then comparing the lists item by item. To do this we have to construct the whole fringe for each tree and turn them both into lists before we can
start the comparison. This may involve a lot of wasted effort, since it may well
be that they differ in their very first elements.

We can produce a much neater solution using processes. We need the following procedures:

```
define fringe(tree);
    vars x;
    if      islist(tree)      ;;; if we have actually got a tree
    then    for x in tree     ;;; we do the same as we did before
            do  fringe(x)
            endfor
    else    x, suspend(1)     ;;; if we have an element of the
    endif;                    ;;; fringe we return it and suspend
enddefine;                    ;;; what we're doing


define genfringe(tree);       ;;; wrap the basic fringe generator up
    fringe(tree);             ;;; in a procedure which returns a
    termin                    ;;; marker when it's finished
enddefine;


define comparefringes(tree1, tree2);
    vars fringe1, fringe2, f1, f2;
    consproc(tree1, 1, genfringe) -> fringe1;
    consproc(tree2, 1, genfringe) -> fringe2;
    ;;; FRINGE1 and FRINGE2 are processes which return the next
    ;;; element of the respective fringes and then suspend
    ;;; themselves. When they have finished they will die
    while   isliveprocess(fringe1)      ;;; check they're both still
            and isliveprocess(fringe2)  ;;; going
    do      runproc(0, fringe1) -> f1;  ;;; get the next element of
            runproc(0, fringe2) -> f2;  ;;; each fringe
            [Next elements are %f1% and %f2%] =>
            unless  f1 = f2             ;;; make sure they're the same
            then    return(false)       ;;; result of overall
            endunless;                  ;;; comparison is FALSE if not
    endwhile;
    not(isliveprocess(fringe1))         ;;; make sure they're both
        and not(isliveprocess(fringe2)) ;;; finished together
enddefine;
```

We will try comparefringes on two simple trees:

```
trace fringe;
```

```
comparefringes([[a b] [c]], [a [[b [c]]]]) =>
> fringe [[a b] [c]]
!> fringe [a b]
!!> fringe a        ;;; the generator for the first tree produces its
                    ;;; first fringe element
> fringe [a [[b [c]]]]
!> fringe a         ;;; the first fringe element of the second tree
** [Next elements are a and a]
!!< fringe
!!> fringe b        ;;; second element of first fringe
!< fringe
   ...
** [Next elements are b and b]
   ...
** [Next elements are c and c]
   ...
** [Next elements are <termin> and <termin>] ;;; final markers
** <true>
```

Now try it on two differing trees:

```
comparefringes([[a b] [c [d e]]], [a [[x [c d]] e]]) =>
> fringe [[a b] [c [d e]]]
!> fringe [a b]
!!> fringe a
> fringe [a [[x [c d]] e]]
!> fringe a
** [Next elements are a and a]
!!< fringe
!!> fringe b        ;;; second element of first fringe
!< fringe
!> fringe [[x [c d]] e]
!!> fringe [x [c d]]
!!!> fringe x        ;;; second element of second fringe
** [Next elements are b and x]
** <false>                    ;;; early report of mismatch
```

Note that in the second example the calls of fringe do not unwind normally. Immediately the mismatch is found, comparefringes exits.

14.5 CONTINUATION PROGRAMMING

Many AI problems involve the exploration of some space of probabilities. During the course of such exploration it is frequently necessary to decide which of several options to investigate. Programs which have to choose between options in this way have to be able to 'backtrack' when their original choice turns out not to lead to a solution. POP-11 provides the facilities needed for a mechanism, called 'continuation programming', for saving decision points so they can be returned to later. Continuation programming is at the heart of the POPLOG version of PROLOG, and has been widely used in AI programs.

In ordinary programming, procedure calls may be seen as requests to achieve sub-tasks. When a sub-task has been successfully performed, control returns to the point where the request was made and continues from there. In continuation programming, procedure calls are still seen as requests to achieve sub-tasks. The difference is that the procedure is explicitly told what should be done next if the sub-task is accomplished. A normal return from a procedure is interpreted as meaning that the task was not successfully completed.

How do we tell a procedure what we want done when it has achieved its goal? We pass it a 'continuation', which is an extra argument which is itself a procedure. This continuation is to be applied when the original procedure has succeeded in its task. The continuation is the specification of what is to be done next.

We will illustrate this idea with a program for answering questions about family relationships. We start by developing procedures which can tell whether one person is an ancestor of another, given a database of facts about who is whose mother or father. The first procedure we need is one for seeing if one person is a parent of another:

```
define parent(continuer, p, c);
    if       present([mother ^p ^c])  ;;; if P is C's mother
    then     continuer()              ;;; then do what was asked for
    endif;
    if       present([father ^p ^c])  ;;; if P is C's father
    then     continuer()              ;;; then do what was asked for
    endif;
enddefine;
```

The interesting thing about this procedure is the presence of the first argument, continuer. parent is a procedure which is to be used by other procedures that know what they want done if parent finds that p is c's mother or father. Here is an example of such a procedure:

```
define ancestor(continuer, a, c);
    vars p;
    parent(continuer, a, c);          ;;; if A is C's parent, then A
                                      ;;; is indeed C's ancestor. So
                                      ;;; do what was asked for next.
    if       present([mother ?p ^c]) ;;; try to find C's mother
    then     ancestor(continuer, a, p) ;;; see if A is her ancestor
    endif;
    if       present([father ?p ^c]) ;;; try to find C's father
    then     ancestor(continuer, a, p) ;;; see if A is his ancestor
    endif;
enddefine;
```

ancestor is another procedure which expects to be given a specification of what is to be done if it is successful. ancestor has three ways of seeing if one person is another's ancestor. First it asks parent to see if a is c's parent. If so, parent will apply the continuation which it inherited from ancestor. If parent returns normally, without applying continuer, ancestor looks in the database for c's mother, and then calls itself recursively to see if a is this person's ancestor. Again a normal return from the recursive call, without continuer being applied, indicates that this attempt to prove the relationship between a and c has failed, so ancestor tries again with c's father. If this last attempt fails, control returns to the procedure that asked whether a was an ancestor of c.

ancestor itself has to be passed a continuation. We can imagine yet more procedures that call ancestor, which themselves have continuations. Where does the original continuation come from? We need to start out with a procedure like the following:

```
define question(what) -> yes_or_no ;
    vars yes_or_no;
    define success();
        true -> yes_or_no; ;;; YES_OR_NO is global to SUCCESS
        exitto(question);
    enddefine;
    false -> yes_or_no; ;;; assume you're going to fail
    what(success);      ;;; call WHAT, with SUCCESS as continuation
enddefine;
```

This is rather intricate. question's argument, what, will be something we want it to investigate for us. This something will be a procedure which takes a continuation. The continuation we are going to supply is the locally defined procedure success. success does two things. It records that the task was successfully accomplished, by switching the value of yes_or_no from false to true; and then it uses exitto to return control directly to question, which immediately exits. success is only called at the point in the investigation where some sub-procedure succeeds, and hence actually calls its continuation. If none of them do, control will eventually return to question in the normal way, but the value of yes_or_no will still be false.

The following shows question being used to interrogate a simple database.

```
vars database;
[[father bob jane]
 [mother peggy jane]
 [father bob lyn]
 [mother peggy lyn]
 [father mike andrew]
 [mother lyn andrew]] -> database;


trace ancestor parent present;

question(ancestor(% "bob", "andrew" %)) =>
> ancestor  <procedure success> bob andrew
!> parent  <procedure success>  bob andrew ;;; is Bob's Andrew's parent
!!> present [mother bob andrew]
!!< present <false>              ;;; not his mother
!!> present [father bob andrew]
!!< present <false>              ;;; not his father
!< parent                       ;;; so PARENT returns - failed
!> present [mother ? p andrew]  ;;; find Andrew's mother - Lyn
!< present <true>
!> ancestor  <procedure success> bob lyn ;;; is Bob Lyn's ancestor?
!!> parent  <procedure success>  bob lyn ;;; well is he her parent?
!!!> present [mother bob lyn]
!!!< present <false>             ;;; isn't her mother
!!!> present [father bob lyn]
!!!< present <true>              ;;; but is her father
** <true>                       ;;; so SUCCESS sets YES_OR_NO to TRUE
                                ;;; and unwinds control to QUESTION


question(ancestor(% "andrew", "jane" %)) =>
> ancestor  <procedure success> andrew jane
!> parent  <procedure success>  andrew jane
   ...
!< parent                       ;;; Andrew is not Jane's parent
!> present [mother ? p jane]     ;;; Who is Jane's mother? - Peggy
!< present <true>
!> ancestor  <procedure success> andrew peggy
!!> parent  <procedure success>  andrew peggy
   ...
!!< parent                       ;;; Andrew is not Peggy's parent
!!> present [mother ? p peggy]  ;;; who is Peggy's mother? - unknown
```

```
!!< present <false>
!!> present [father ? p peggy]   ;;; who is Peggy's father? - unknown
!!< present <false>
!< ancestor                      ;;; Andrew is not Peggy's ancestor
!> present [father ? p jane]     ;;; who is Jane's father? - Bob
!< present <true>
!> ancestor   <procedure success> andrew bob
    ...
!< ancestor                      ;;; Andrew is not Bob's ancestor
< ancestor                       ;;; original call of ANCESTOR returns
** <false>                       ;;; normally with YES_OR_NO still FALSE
```

This mechanism makes use of the ordinary POP-11 calling stack for storing the decision points. This is rather more efficient than using an explicit data structure, such as a list, for storing them. The great advantage of continuation programming over other ways of using the calling stack for saving decision points is that it does not interfere with its normal use for looking after procedure calls. In particular, there is no problem with using recursive procedures with continuations.

There is one further complication to be dealt with. In the family tree example we had several alternative ways in which one person could be another's ancestor. The alternatives were explored in sequence, with each option represented by an individual procedure call. What are we going to do about situations where we have several sub-tasks which must all be achieved together? For instance, how could we define a procedure to find out if two people are siblings (brother or sister), using the fact that people are siblings if they have the same parents? The following procedure will do it for us:

```
define sibling(continuer, a, b);
    vars f m;
    if      present([father ?f ^a])     ;;; Get A's mother and father
            and present([mother ?m ^a])
    then    parent(parent(% continuer, f, b %), m, b)
    endif;
enddefine;
```

In this procedure, we look up a's parents quite straightforwardly. We then ask parent to see if a's mother is a parent of b. If she is, we want to continue by seeing if a's father is also a parent of b, and only if he is should sibling's original continuation be called.

```
trace sibling parent present;

question(sibling(% "jane", "lyn" %)) =>
> sibling <procedure success> jane lyn
!> present [father ? f jane] ;;; get Jane's father - Bob
!< present <true>
!> present [mother ? m jane] ;;; and her mother - Peggy
!< present <true>
!> parent <procedure parent> peggy lyn  ;;; is Peggy Lyn's parent?
!!> present [mother peggy lyn]
```

```
!!< present <true>                          ;;; yes
!!> parent <procedure success> bob lyn  ;;; is Bob Lyn's parent?
!!!> present [mother bob lyn]
!!!< present <false>
!!!> present [father bob lyn]
!!!< present <true>                         ;;; yes
** <true>                                   ;;; so successful exit
```

We have seen how to use continuation programming to implement back-tracking in a problem where we may have sets of sub-goals which are alternatives, or sets of sub-goals which must all be achieved together. We deal with alternatives by writing them in sequence; we deal with simultaneous sub-goals by embodying the later goal as part of the continuation of the earlier one, with the continuation that was passed into the first goal passed on by freezing it into the second one.

The example does not discuss how to pass results other than true or false out when a successful conclusion is reached. In general this can be quite tricky if the result is to be built up out of components which are obtained at various levels in a recursive search of a space. We will leave this as a final, hard, exercise. If you manage to find a solution, you can shut this book with full confidence that you have learnt POP-11.

Exercise

3. Using continuation programming, write procedures which can answer the following questions:

> "Who are the descendants of Bob?"
> "Who are the siblings of Lyn?"
> "Who are the ancestors of Andrew?"

Appendix: Syntax diagrams

Expression

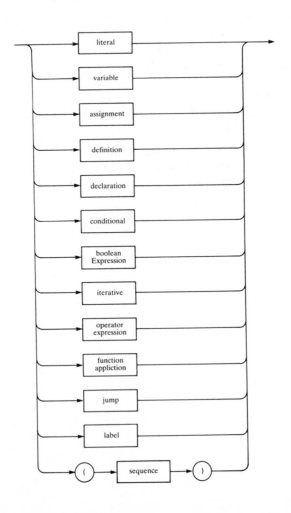

Definition

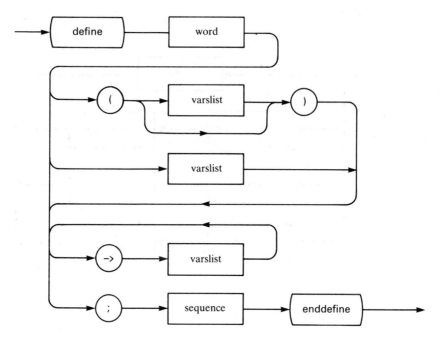

Assignment

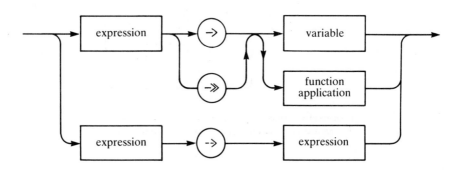

Variable

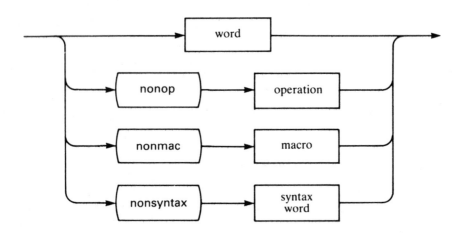

Declaration

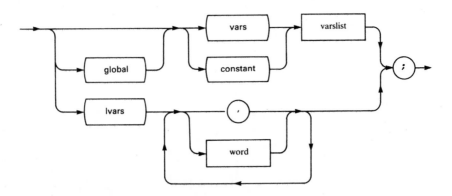

(i)   constant declarations may not appear inside procedure definitions
(ii) lvars declarations may not appear outside procedure definitions

Varslist

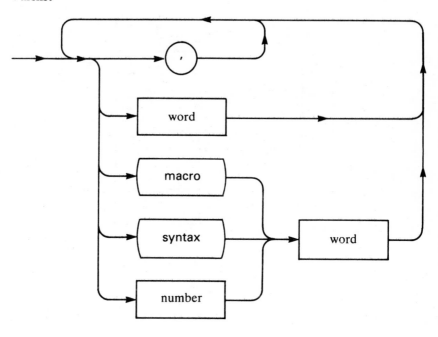

The bottom three options would not commonly be used in procedure headings

Sequence

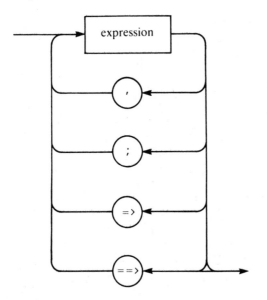

Literal

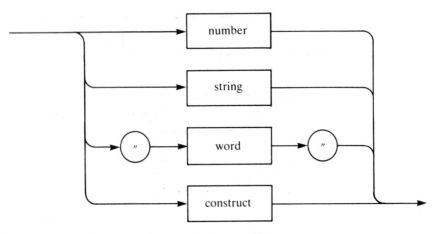

Construct

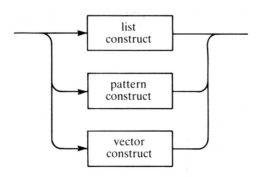

Vector construct

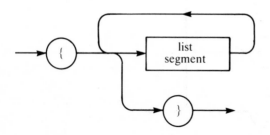

List construct

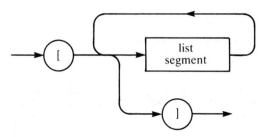

Pattern construct

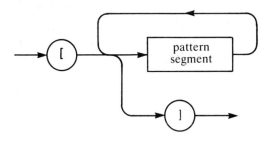

List Segment

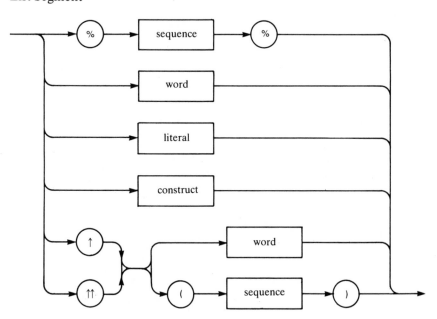

Pattern segment

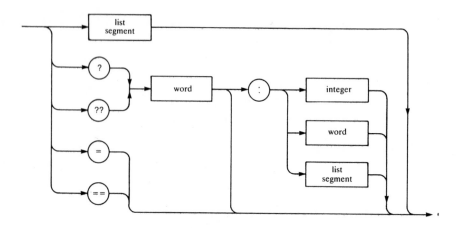

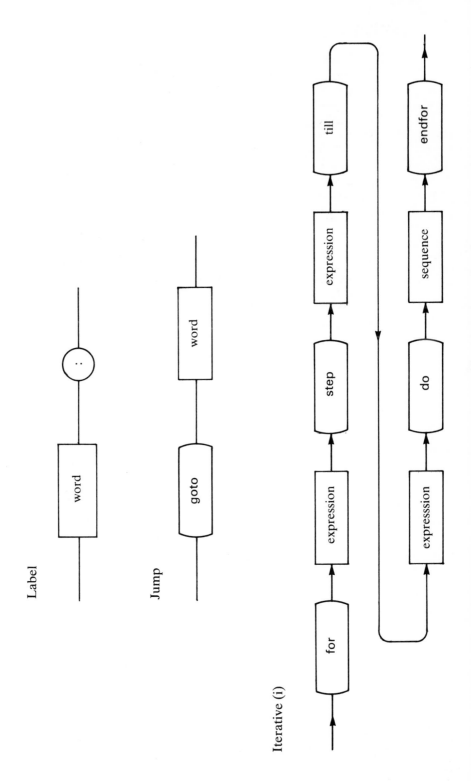

Label

Jump

Iterative (i)

Iterative (ii)

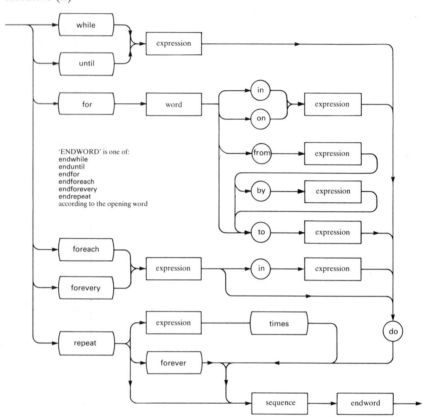

'ENDWORD' is one of:
endwhile
enduntil
endfor
endforeach
endforevery
endrepeat
according to the opening word

Conditional

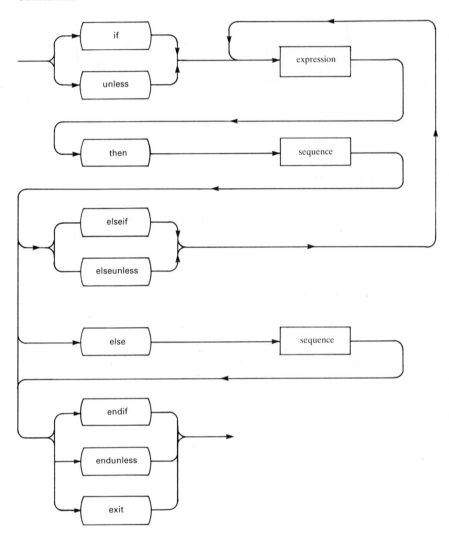

Boolean expression

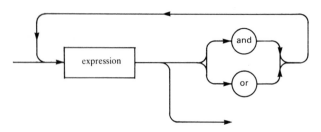

Operator expression

Function application

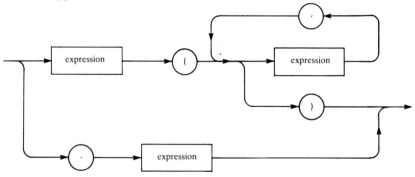

Answers to exercises

1 A DETAILED WORKED EXAMPLE

1. display_room needs to be modified in order that the dimensions of a room be printed out before the perimeter, with something like the following inserted into the procedure:

```
pr(' dimensions are '); pr(list(2)); pr(' by ');
pr(list(3)); pr(' by '); pr(list(4)); pr(newline);
```

2. The for . . . endfor loop does something with each element of a list in turn.
3. A local variable is declared inside a procedure.
   A global variable is declared outside a procedure.
4. len, breadth, height, area(len, breadth), area(len, breadth) * height
5. In a procedure heading —> does not cause an assignment. It indicates that a procedure will produce a result. The result is the value of the output variable at the point when the procedure exits. In an assignment —> assigns whatever is on the left of the arrow to whatever is on the right of the arrow.
6. findroom_len can be based on display_data, slightly modified so that information about all rooms of a specified length is printed out:

```
define findroom_len(len, list_of_lists);
    vars room;
    for room in list_of_lists do
        if room(2) = len then display_room(room) endif;
    endfor;
enddefine;
```

```
7. define find_and_show_all(namelist, list_of_lists);
        vars room;
        for room in list_of_lists do
             if member(room(1), namelist) then display_room(room); endif;
        endfor;
    enddefine;
```

2 SYNTAX AND SEMANTICS OF POP-11

1. Expressions in POP-11 refer to objects.
2. Imperatives in POP-11 refer to actions.
3. POP-11 objects include numbers, words, lists, strings.
4. => prints items
   addup(num); runs the procedure addup with num as input
   26 —> num; assigns 26 to the variable num
   vars x ; declares x as a variable name to POP-11

5.
```
    define addmult(x, y, z) -> result;
        ;;; adds X and Y, then multiplies by Z
        (x + y) * z -> result;
    enddefine;
```

6. Defining a procedure declares the procedure name as a variable and assigns the instructions in the procedure to it.
   Calling a procedure means that the instructions are obeyed.
7. Procedures may be called with input. For example, a procedure defined to add up a list of numbers, named addup, needs to be given a list of numbers as input, as in:

```
addup([1 2 3 4]);
```

Procedures do not have to take input arguments. It will not be necessary in printing procedures, for example:

```
define print_out();
    pr('no input arguments');
enddefine;
```

Not all procedures produce results. print_out does not. It prints the characters in the string out on the terminal screen.
8. The pretty print arrow, ==>, prints only one object. It uses a special printing format for clarity if the object extends over more than one line.
   The ordinary print arrow, =>, prints everything on the stack unless called from inside a procedure, when it prints only the top item. It does not have a special print format for clarity.
9. A comment indicates that the proceeding text must be ignored by the compiler. The text is inserted in programs for explanatory purposes. Short comments follow three consecutive semicolons ;;;. Longer comments are put in between /* and */.

10. 99100 101102 103
11. Predicates are procedures which produce a boolean result. The if part of a condition must always evaluate to either <true> or <false>. This determines executing the <action> part.
12. (i) yes; (ii) no; (iii) yes; (iv) no; (v) yes; (vi) yes.

3 THE STACK

1. i. ** [a b c]; ii. ** [a b c]; iii. ** [a b c]; iv. ** y

2. (((2 + 3) * 4) + 5) − 2 => denotes 23
    (i) put 2 on the stack
    (ii) put 3 on the stack
    (iii) do the addition
    (iv) put 4 on the stack
    (v) do the multiplication
    (vi) put 5 on the stack
    (vii) do the addition
    (viii) put 2 on the stack
    (ix) do the subtraction
    (x) print out the contents of the stack.

3. (i)
```
1, 2, 3, 4;
-> x;
=>
** 1 2 3
x =>
** 4
```
(ii)
```
1, 2, 3, 4;
->> x;
=>
** 1 2 3 4
x =>
** 4
```

4. (i) 4; (ii) 1 2 3 4; (iii) 4.
5. ** 6 7 6 10
6. erase(18 // 4) =>

4 ARITHMETIC

1. (i) integer; (ii) ddecimal; (iii) word; (iv) string; (v) list (or pair).
2. (i) 36; (ii) 23; (iii) 35; (iv) 3.0; (v) 1.
3. The variable popradians controls whether the trigonometric procedures take arguments, or produce results, in degrees (if its value is <false>) or radians (if its value is <true>).
4. Assign 16 to pop_pr_radix to make POP-11 print in hexadecimal form.

5.
```
define new_random() -> r;
    (random(536870910) / 268435455) -1 -> r;
enddefine;
```

5 LISTS

1. (i) [[[a]]]

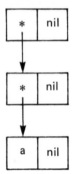

(ii) [a [b [c [d]]]]

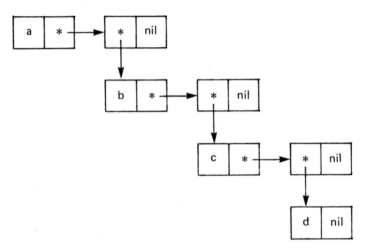

2.
```
define list_nums_to(n) -> list;
    vars num;
    [] -> list;
    for num from 1 to n do
        [^^list ^num] -> list;   ;;; this line is different
    endfor;
enddefine;
```

3. [sam is a ^(hd(x))]

   is

   [sam is a cat]

   This could be achieved with ^^ by doing:

   [sam is a ^^x] =>

4. i. [3 4 5 6]; ii. [this is a list of words]; iii. [2 is the only
number in this list]; iv. [[this is one list of words] [and this is
another]]; v. [[456 7 8 8 [34 556 2345] 788 4 5]].

5. (i) once; (ii) lamb; (iii) [mary had] ; (iv) [lamb little a had mary] ; (v) had;
   (vi) [mouse pig dog] ; (vii) brown; (viii) white; (ix) tom; (x) [mary green] ;
   (xi) [brown] ; (xii) [[suzy white]] .

6. oneof takes a list as argument and produces an element from the list chosen
   randomly.

7. delete usually takes two input arguments, any item, and a list. It produces
   the list minus whatever the item was. delete produces an empty list if the
   second argument contains only occurrences of the first argument. To stop
   delete deleting all the found items, give it an extra argument specifying how
   many to delete.

8. (i) [5 4 2 1] ; (ii) [lamb a had mary] .

9.
```
define deal(pack,num);
     vars card;
     repeat num times
        oneof(pack) -> card;        ;;; select a card
        delete(card,pack) -> pack;  ;;; remove it from the pack
        card =>                     ;;; print it out
     endrepeat;
enddefine;
```

This procedure takes two arguments, a list and a number. It does some
printing, but does not produce a result. That is to say, the things printed
out are not left on the stack; card is used as a local variable, which temporarily stores the selected card. Notice that the line

```
delete(card,pack) -> pack;
```

alters the value of the variable pack so that it refers to a list no longer
containing the card. The next time round the loop the card will not be
selected. Although that line removes the card from the list, it is still the
value of the variable card, so that it can be printed out in the next line.

```
card =>
```

We can test this with a pack of 12 cards, from which we want 6 dealt.
We use s1 for ace of spades, h2 for two of hearts, etc.

```
deal( [ s1 s2 s3 h1 h2 h3 d1 d2 d3 c1 c2 c3 ] , 6);
** s1
** d2
** s2
** s3
** h1
** h3
```

Note that this definition of deal assumes that no card occurs twice in the
pack. delete could be given a third argument to make it delete one occurrence only.

10.
```
(i)     [i love my] -> x; [] -> y;
(ii)    [6 ft] -> x;
(iii)   [fire man] -> x; [civil servant] -> y;
(iv)    Impossible
(v)     [sometimes] -> x; [hate people like] -> y;
(vi)    "a" -> x; [b c d] -> y; [] -> z;
(vii)   [a b] -> x; [c d] -> y; [e f] -> z;
```

```
(viii)   [3] -> n;
(ix)     3 -> n;
(x)      Impossible
(xi)     "i" -> x; "hate" -> y; "computers" -> z;
```

6 PROCEDURES AND OTHER CONTROL FACILITIES

1.
```
define len(list) ->r;
     vars item;
     0 -> r;
     for item in list do
         1 + r -> r;
     endfor;
enddefine;
```

2.
```
define trans(inches) -> inc -> feet;
     if inches < 12 then
         0 -> feet; inches -> inc;
     elseif inches > 12 then
         inches div 12 -> feet; inches rem 12 -> inc;
     else
         1 -> feet; 0 -> inc;
     endif;
enddefine;
```

trans could have been defined more efficiently thus:

```
define trans2(inches) -> inc -> feet;
     inches // 12 -> feet -> inc;
enddefine;
```

3. The <action> in the while loop is performed as long as the <condition> is not <false>
The <action> in the until loop is performed as long as the <condition> is <false>.

4.
```
vars num;
1 -> num;
while num * num < 100 do
    num + 1 -> num;
endwhile;

vars num; 1 -> num;
until num * num >= 100 do
    num + 1 -> num;
enduntil;
```

5.
```
vars item x; [1 2 3 4] -> x;
for item on x do tl(item) => endfor;
** [2 3 4]
** [3 4]
** [4]
** []
```

```
6.  define myrev(list) -> out;
        vars item;
        [] -> out;
        for item in list do
            [^item ^^out] -> out;
        endfor;
    enddefine;
```

7 RECURSION

```
1.  define delete(item, list) -> result;
        if list = [] then [] ;;; stopping condition
        elseif
            hd(list) = item then   ;;; do not want item in new
            delete(item, tl(list));  ;;; list so ignore it
        else
            hd(list) :: delete(item, tl(list));
        endif -> result;
    enddefine;
```

```
2.  define rec_rev(list) -> result; ;;; not embedded as in [1 2 3 4]
        if list = [] then []
        else
            [^^(rec_rev(tl(list))) ^(hd(list))]; ;;; builds the list
        endif -> result;                         ;;; backwards
    enddefine;
```

```
3.  define recursive_rev(list) -> result;
        if list = [] then []
        elseif islist(hd(list)) then
            [^^(recursive_rev(tl(list))) ^(recursive_rev(hd(list)))];
        else
            [^^(recursive_rev(tl(list))) ^(hd(list))];
        endif -> result;
    enddefine;
```

Alternatively, using atom, recursive_rev could have been defined as:

```
define recursive_rev(list) -> result;
    if atom(list) then
        list
    else
        [^^(recursive_rev(tl(list))) ^(recursive_rev(hd(list)))]
    endif -> result
enddefine;
```

8 THE POP-11 MATCHER

1. (i) <true> (ii) <true>
2. i.
```
    define headlist(x)-> result;
        x --> [?result ==]
    enddefine;
```
   ii.
```
    define taillist(x) -> result;
        x --> [= ??result]
    enddefine;
```

3.

(i) [i love my mother] matches [??x mother ??y] => ** <true>
x => ** [i love my]
y => ** []

(ii) [the height of steve is 6 ft]
matches [the height of steve is ??x] => ** <true>
x => ** [6 ft]

(iii) [every fire man is a civil servant]
matches [every ??x is a ??y] => ** <true>
x => ** [fire man]
y => ** [civil servant]

(iv) [every fire man is a civil servant]
matches [every ^x is a ^y] => ** <false>

(v) [sometimes i hate people like you] matches [??x i ??y you] =>
** <true>
x => ** [sometimes]   y => ** [hate people like]

(vi) [[a b c d]] matches [[?x ??y] ??z] =>
** <true>
x => ** a
y => ** [b c d]
z => ** []

(vii) [[a b] [c d] [e f]] matches [?x [??y] ?z] =>
** <true> x => ** [a b]
y => ** [c d]
z => ** [e f]

(viii)[i saw 3 ships] matches [i saw ??n ships] =>
** <true> n => ** [3]

(ix) [i saw 3 ships] matches [i saw ?n ships] =>
** <true> n => ** 3

(x) [i hate computers] matches [i ?x you] => ** <false>

(xi) [i hate computers] matches [?x ?y ?z] => ** <true>
x => ** i
y => ** hate
z => ** computers

4. To solve 4, we need some new procedures. adjseq will match any sequence
of adjectives, including none. adjseq always succeeds — if the next word is
not an adjective, adjseq returns nil. simple_noun phrase is the same as the
original definition of noun phrase, except that it makes use of adjseq rather
than trying to count adjectives for itself. prepositional phrase matches a
preposition followed by a simple noun phrase. noun phrase now matches
either a simple noun phrase followed by a prepositional phrase, or just a
simple noun phrase.

```
define adjseq(text);
    vars a aseq;
    if      text matches [?a:adjective ??aseq:adjseq]
    then    [^a ^^aseq]
```

```
        else    nil
        endif;
    enddefine;


define simple_noun_phrase(text);
    vars d aseq n;
    if      text matches [?d:determiner ??aseq:adjseq ?n:noun ==]
    then    [NP ^d ^aseq ^n]
    else    false
    endif;
enddefine;

define prepositional_phrase(text);
    vars p NP;
    if      text matches [?p:preposition ??NP:simple_noun_phrase ==]
    then    [PP ^p ^NP]
    else    false
    endif;
enddefine;

define noun_phrase(text);
    vars NP PP;
    if      text matches [??NP:simple_noun_phrase
                          ??PP:prepositional_phrase
                          ==]
    then    [NP ^NP ^PP]
    elseif  text matches [??NP:simple_noun_phrase]
    then    NP
    else    false
    endif;
enddefine;
```

9 THE POP–11 DATABASE

1. present takes one pattern as argument. It returns a boolean expression. We would get a mishap if we typed

   `if present([== a]) then => endif;`

   because the result of present is removed from the stack leaving no arguments for $=>$. We can overcome this by making sure that we do give $=>$ something to print out.
2. present looks for only one matching item. foreach looks for all items matching some pattern and does something to them.
3. We would use lookup. This differs from present because it does not return a boolean expression. It just instantiates variables when a match is found, and produces a mishap if a match is not found.
4. You could use allpresent to see if several patterns are present in the database. The matching items are assigned to the variable them.
5. forevery looks for all possible ways of matching a list of patterns against the database and does something to them. allpresent tries to find just one way and returns a boolean.
6. This is left up to you.

10 ADDITIONAL POP-11 DATA STRUCTURES

1. ```
vars vec;
{this is a vector} -> vec;

"what" -> subscrv(1, vec);
"what" -> vec(1);
```

2. `** <mystring 121 101>`

3. Possible answer:

   ```
   recordclass constant route froma tob road distance direction;

   vars London_Brighton Brighton_Lewes Lewes_T_Wells;

   consroute("Brighton", "London", "A23", 50, "north")
                                   -> London_Brighton;

   consroute( "Brighton", "Lewes", "A27", 8, "east")
                                   -> Brighton_Lewes;

   consroute("Lewes", "Tunbridge_Wells", "A26", 25, "north_east")
                                   -> Lewes_T_Wells;
   ```

4. (i) 2
   (ii) 1 and 4 are the lower and upper bounds for the first dimension, 1 and 6 for the second.
   (iii) 26 (including two words for the length and key fields).

5. i. ```
      {undef undef undef undef undef undef undef undef undef undef
            undef undef undef undef undef}
      ```
   ii.  14 6

6. ```
   vars bad_array;
   newanyarray([1 5 3 6], mult, inits, subscrs, false)
                                   -> bad_array;
   ```

7. ```
   define printarray(array);
       vars bounds row column;
       boundslist(array) -> bounds;
       for row from bounds(1) to bounds(2) do
           for column from bounds(3) to bounds(4) do
               pr(array(row, column)); pr(tab);
           endfor;
           pr(newline);
       endfor;
   enddefine;
   ```

8. ```
   define newassoc(list);
       newproperty(list, 20, false, true);
   enddefine;
   ```

9. Possible answers:
   ```
   define countup(item, value);
       1 + result -> result;
   enddefine;
   ```
   ```

```
    define count_opp -> result;
        0 -> result;
        appproperty(opposite, countup);
    enddefine;
```

ii.
```
    define count_opp -> result;
        0 -> result;
        appproperty(opposite, procedure(i,v); 1 + result -> result
            endprocedure)
    enddefine;
```

10. Dynamic lists are expanded as they are needed.
    They save space and time.
    They can be infinitely long.
    They can contain values unknown at the time of construction.
11. catlist will be expanded infinitely, so this command will never return — it will keep trying to get the last element of catlist so it can return its count of how many items there are in catlist; but there is no last item in catlist, so it will never get there.

11 PROCEDURES REVISITED

1.
```
findone(%iscolour%) -> getcolour;
```

2.
```
define updaterof iscolour(bool, colour);
    if bool then
        colour :: frozval(1, iscolour)
    else
        delete(colour, frozval(1, iscolour));
    endif -> frozval(1, iscolour);
enddefine;
```

12 INPUT/OUTPUT

1. A character repeater is a procedure that reads characters from somewhere and puts them on the stack. It takes no input arguments. charin and procedures produced by discin are character repeaters.
2. Character consumers output characters to somewhere. charout and procedures produced by discout are character consumers.
3. charout.
4. (i) 116 and nothing on the stack
   (ii) 74 and <undef ulia> on the stack
   (iii) t, and nothing on the stack
   (iv) Julia, and nothing on the stack.

5.
```
define char_file_file(fromfile, tofile);
    vars charrep charcon character;
    discout(tofile) -> charcon; ;;; output goes to file
```

```
        discin(fromfile) -> charrep; ;;; read input from file
        until (charrep() ->> character) = termin do
            charcon(character);
        enduntil;
        pr(termin); ;;; this closes the file
    enddefine;
```

6. ```
   define showfile(file);
       vars charrep character;
       discin(file) -> charrep; ;;; makes a character repeater
       until (charrep() ->> character) = termin do
           cucharout(character);
       enduntil;
   enddefine;
   ```

7. A break character is one which, when detected by the operating system, causes it to empty its input buffer by sending its contents to the receiving programs.

8. popdevin and popdevout are non-raw buffered devices.
   popdevraw is a raw buffered device.

9. ```
   vars buffer;
   [] -> buffer;

   define buffercharout(char, charrep);
       if length(buffer) = 128 then
           applist(buffer, charrep);
           [] -> buffer; ;;; flush the buffer
       endif;
       [^^buffer ^char] -> buffer;
   enddefine;

   buffercharout(%charout%) -> cucharout;
   ```

13 THE POP-11 COMPILER

1. `pdtolist(incharitem(cucharin)) —> proglist;`
2. When VM code is complete for a single procedure.
3. Syntax procedures are written directly using VM code-planting procedures. Thus proglist is not changed. Syntax procedures are run at compile time, macros at read time.
4. ```
   vars macro fild;
       [vars item; for item in list do] —> nonmac fild;

   vars macro efild;
       [endfor;] —> nonmac efild;

   len([1 2 3 4 9]) =>
   ** 5

   len([]) =>
   ** 0
   ```
   ```

14 NON-STANDARD CONTROL STRUCTURES

1.
```
define next2(n);
    repeat forever
        n, ksuspend(1);  ;;; process will die after being run once
        n - 1 -> n;
    endrepeat;
enddefine;

vars process;
23, consproc(1, next2) -> process;

runproc(0, process) =>
** 23
```

If you try to run it again, for example with

```
runproc(0, process) =>
```

the system will print out the following mishap message:

```
;;; MISHAP - ATTEMPT TO RUN DEAD PROCESS
;;; INVOLVING:  <process>
;;; DOING    :  runproc compile nextitem compile
```

2.
```
1,1
2,

;;; MISHAP - ATTEMPT TO RUN DEAD PROCESS
;;; INVOLVING:  <process>
;;; DOING    :  runproc procedure1 runproc compile nextitem compile
```

3. Is left entirely up to you.

Index